MW00943606

LAST CALL

Twelve Men Who Dared Answer

Edited by Ronda Chervin, Ph.D.

They shall bring forth fruit even in old age, still full of sap, still green.
Ps. 92: 14

Last Call
Twelve Men Who Dared Answer

Copyright © 2012 by Ronda Chervin, Ph.D.

Design by James Kent Ridley

Published by Goodbooks Media

ISBN-13: 978-1478162735
ISBN-10: 1478162732

Ut in Omnes Gloriam Deum

GOODBOOKS MEDIA

God sought me out when I fled from Him;
He will not abandon me now that I seek Him,
or at least flee from Him any more.
St. Claude de la Colombiére

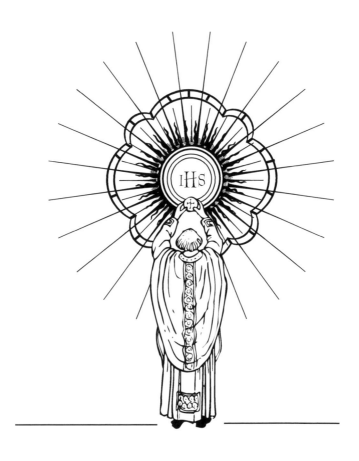

CONTENTS

Concerning Holy Apostles College and Seminary

Holy Apostles Seminary, Cromwell, Connecticut was founded on July 10, 1957, by a French Canadian Franciscan, Rev. Eusebe M. Menard, OFM, for the promotion of belated vocations to the Roman Catholic priesthood. This was the first seminary in the United States dedicated to the formation of older priestly vocations.

What were the requirements for admission as a belated seminarian? According to the "Decree of the Bishop of Norwich Concerning the Establishment in His Diocese of a Seminary for Belated Vocations to the Priesthood," Holy Apostles Seminary was permitted to accept "only young men of seventeen or older who come from good families and who give serious indications of a priestly vocation."

From a contemporary perspective it is surprising to realize that "belated" in 1957 meant seventeen years of age or older! It was then very common in America for future priests to enter a high school seminary at the age of fourteen. Today the average age of ordination for a priest is thirty-five. Father Menard's vision proved to be prophetic indeed!

The vocational journey of each priest is a unique and precious manifestation of grace at work. A man does not decide on his own to become a priest, but rather answers a personal call from Christ that is authenticated by the Church. Holy Apostles Seminary continues to welcome belated vocations as do most seminaries. This inspiring book, under the guidance of Dr. Ronda Chervin, Professor of Philosophy at Holy Apostles, is a testimony to the legacy of Father Menard, the father of belated vocations to the priesthood in the United States.

Rev. Douglas L. Mosey, CSB, Rector

INTRODUCTION

Last call? Late vocations? Men who dare? Woman editor? What can this be?

My part of the story began in 1987 when, after years of teaching undergraduates, I was privileged to teach philosophy at the seminary of the Archdiocese of Los Angeles. I was hired specifically to teach the men who had college and advanced degrees, but who lacked the ten courses in philosophy required for theological studies.

Feeling that priests are almost an endangered species, I was thrilled to see the men who dared to answer the call of Jesus so that we lay people might be fed our celestial bread. When some feminists talked about hating to see priests concelebrating—all that patriarchy!—I would reply, "Strange you say that. I feel like a queen whose slaves are coming to serve me a banquet." After all, at daily Mass, I don't have to be there, but they do. As a convert from an atheistic though Jewish background, I think of priests as thousands of fathers laying down their lives to serve me.

Teaching at the seminary was one of the best experiences in my life. I loved the variety of these men, ranging in age from late twenties up to the sixties and whose previous professions included engineers, stockbrokers and popular singers. Judged more on character than on grades, these men would vie to prove their virtue publicly in ways delightfully beneficial to the professors. For instance, if I dropped a hankie four men would leap to fetch it!

The job was a perfect fit for me because my gift is to synthesize philosophy, spirituality and psychology. Most late-vocation seminarians come in a bit frightened of philosophy, so a mix with spirituality and psychology makes the subject less intimidating.

After becoming a widow in 1993, I taught in other places, but by 1999-2002, I was teaching older seminarians again. This was at the small, emerging college of Our Lady of Corpus Christi in Texas, run by the Society of Our Lady of the Most Holy Trinity (SOLT). These daring men I also loved and admired. Older myself, I could only imagine how much love for Jesus and the Church it would take to be willing to sit in a classroom again for four to six years!

After many other teaching adventures, now, in 2010, I am offering philosophy courses to seminarians at Holy Apostles College and Seminary in Connecticut. This seminary was founded in the 1950s by the Missionaries of the Holy Apostles whose Canadian founder, Fr. Eusebe Menard, was convinced that there was a need for a seminary designed for late-vocation priests.

More than a thousand men ranging from their twenties to mid-seventies at ordination have been trained at Holy Apostles. Thankfully, many more dioceses now also ordain men in their later years.

Right now, I live on the grounds of the seminary where I participate in morning prayer, Mass, evening prayer and meals with the seminarians. Gradually, I have come to know the stories of these daring men, some of whom have come from distant lands, such as North Vietnam, Lebanon, South America and Canada. Those who are American-born include a variety of backgrounds as well: Puerto Rican, Nigerian, English, South American, Chinese, Polish, Filipino, Asian Indian, Ukrainian, as well as French, Irish, German, and Italian. I have always found the Catholic Church to be the true "United Nations."

Their previous occupations are just as varied. These men have had careers in law enforcement, music, computer science, politics, military service, carpentry, international business, psychotherapy, and education. Some have always been single. Some have been religious brothers. Some were married and obtained annulments. Some are widowers. Most are headed to the diocesan priesthood but some belong to religious communities.

All of the men whose vocation stories are featured in this book feel unworthy of so exalted a vocation. All of them regret to think of other Catholic men whom God may be calling but lack the courage or support to make a response. These men hope that their stories will move you to consider what might be your last chance at such a fulfilling a choice. They hope that all Catholics reading these stories may be encouraged by the sign of each priestly vocation, and see in them the unique provision of our Lord, who will not allow the gates of hell to prevail.

In closing I want to acknowledge with deep gratitude Elizabeth Hanink, who kindly undertook the editing of the first version of this manuscript; and James Ridley, who created with great skill the cover and interior design of this book.

Ronda Chervin, PhD

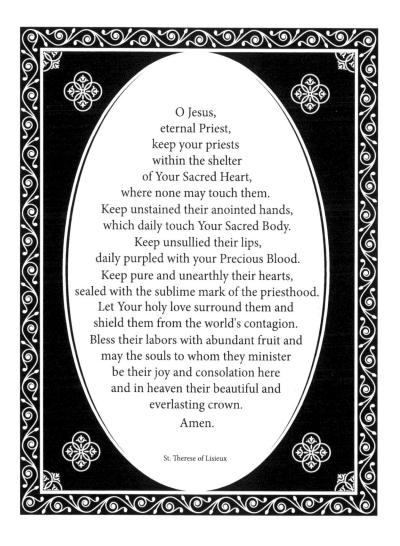

O Jesus,
eternal Priest,
keep your priests
within the shelter
of Your Sacred Heart,
where none may touch them.
Keep unstained their anointed hands,
which daily touch Your Sacred Body.
Keep unsullied their lips,
daily purpled with your Precious Blood.
Keep pure and unearthly their hearts,
sealed with the sublime mark of the priesthood.
Let Your holy love surround them and
shield them from the world's contagion.
Bless their labors with abundant fruit and
may the souls to whom they minister
be their joy and consolation here
and in heaven their beautiful and
everlasting crown.
Amen.

St. Therese of Lisieux

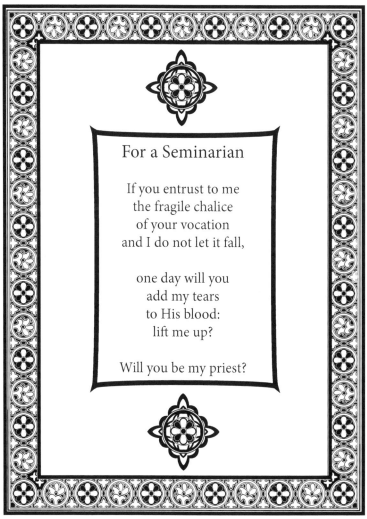

For a Seminarian

If you entrust to me
the fragile chalice
of your vocation
and I do not let it fall,

one day will you
add my tears
to His blood:
lift me up?

Will you be my priest?

Ronda Chervin

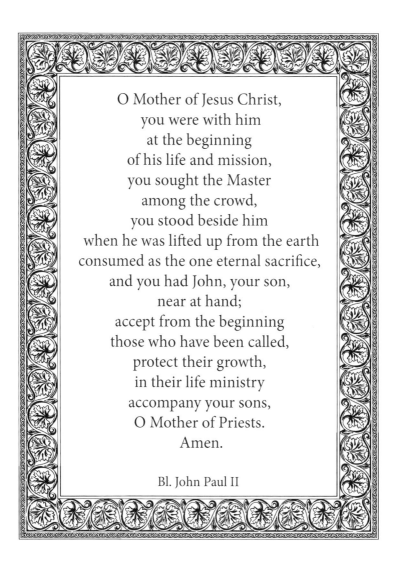

O Mother of Jesus Christ,
you were with him
at the beginning
of his life and mission,
you sought the Master
among the crowd,
you stood beside him
when he was lifted up from the earth
consumed as the one eternal sacrifice,
and you had John, your son,
near at hand;
accept from the beginning
those who have been called,
protect their growth,
in their life ministry
accompany your sons,
O Mother of Priests.
Amen.

Bl. John Paul II

Back to My Senses:
the Faith, the Church, and the Priesthood

Br. Jeffrey "Skip" Thompson, M.S.A.

The strength of God's mercy that comes when we courageously confront our own sinfulness is a powerful undercurrent in this story. Great tragedies and great sorrows need not defeat us in our quest for lasting peace with Him.

The nice thing about destroying one's life is the opportunity it presents for beginning a new one. In the spring of 2002, the pastor of the Baptist church I attended recommended a fine Christian counselor to me. I had experienced a prodigal son crash-and-burn from the heights of worldly success and needed a Christian who was a trained and neutral party to advise me how to sort through the wreckage, spiritual and otherwise. Ironically, it was pain, mostly of the self-inflicted variety, that had awakened me to my spiritual senses. With desperate intensity I grasped for the God who was for me and not against me and decided to cooperate with God and faith again. For two or three visits my counselor rarely spoke, but listened attentively to my life story. Finally he stated, "Few men have the chance to completely restart their lives, but you are one of them."

I was baptized Roman Catholic as an infant but left the Church shortly after Confirmation. The Latin Mass was unintelligible to me and thus the Church seemed irrelevant to real life, especially the life that interested a thirteen-year-old. The Church seemed more about human rules than a relationship with God, which was how I would later explain my departure. Nonetheless, I believe the grace of the sacraments followed me to college where I responded to a Christian outreach on campus and made a conscious commitment to Christ. I was promised that God had a wonderful plan for my life, which sounded great. I wanted a wonderful plan for life and had no clue about how to get it. My Catholic upbringing had never presented faith as tantalizing and as simply as this. Consequently, I fell out of the Barque of Peter and into a Protestant lifeboat.

From this Protestant para-church reintroduction to Christianity, I began to investigate various denominations in order to call one my own. I dove into the new theological waters with faith that the Holy Spirit would guide my search. Among my explorations were Pentecostal, Lutheran, Reformed and Baptist churches. Only in America is such spiritual shopping available, and at the time I had no idea how historically unique this is. But I trusted that someone, somewhere, had researched and could recommend the true faith. Discovering the best reformed Christian "product" seemed just a matter of seeking.

However, it soon became evident there was nothing clear about Protestant theology. There was, though, a pattern. The origins of various denominations lay in institutionalized personality cults. Successful movements had sprung up all over the map, but their only common denominator was that they were not Catholic. I presumed that so many denominations meant the Holy Spirit needed to move the Catholic Church back to the straight and narrow and that the Church was no longer united under a single authority. Curiously, I was also finding that Protestant denominations, though all claiming to base their authority on the Reformation tradition of *sola scriptura* (the Bible alone) as the rule of faith, nonetheless disputed one another's interpretations. From Luther and Zwingli's first falling out to the present day, theologically and ecclesiastically speaking, the straight and narrow was more like fractured and obscure.

Regardless of these reservations, I attended a nondenominational church while in college and upon graduation from the University of California, Davis, seriously considered applying for seminary training. My denominational search continued, but I gave pride of place to reformed theology, which seemed the most venerable of non-Catholic offerings. It became imperative to settle the denominational question before entering a seminary, so I interviewed several pastors, including a Catholic priest, to ascertain the best way to go about it. Each advised me that he had been born into his denomination and never gave the question another thought. But each pastor also advised me to get some real-world experience before entering. That seemed to me a wise course of action.

Why I discussed my ministry interest with a priest I don't really know; call it an attempt at objectivity, or perhaps an unconscious foreshadowing. I considered the Catholic priesthood with its requirement of chastity a form of unrealistic starvation for a young male and never seriously considered re-entering the Church, let alone her ministry. I had a very wrong view of Catholicism, but I did not honestly examine that view for many years.

Toward the goal of real-life experience, I found work in Sacramento at the state capitol of California, and I sought a wife. I married a wonderful Christian girl, and all was love and happiness for a few short years. As my career began to flourish, an unexpected abyss awaited in 1983.

Shortly after giving birth to our son, my wife succumbed to postpartum psychosis, a phenomenon that can drastically alter a new mother's brain chemistry due to massive hormonal shifts associated with childbirth. In her diminished mental state she killed our child and was arrested for murder. The event was unfathomable.

For the next few months I functioned, but in a surreal world in which I awoke daily to find my nightmare was real. Stunned, devastated, and angry, I questioned the goodness of God, who seemed to sit idly by while the unimaginable happened to my family. Why? I could not process these events. No theology could explain our fiasco so I abandoned my trust in God, who appeared to offer no defense against evil's ill designs. My life seemed to contradict directly the great Psalms that laud Him as protector and shield. On the contrary, God seemed aloof and uncaring. So much for the wonderful plan for my life.

I listened to the devil's ancient lies concerning God's love and intentions, and instead of Christ, turned to my own speculations about life. I wallowed in my supposed ill-treatment as His child. If God didn't care about my life, I was free to ignore Him as well. I stopped attending our little reformed church and any church whatsoever.

I arranged for a good criminal lawyer and my wife stood trial for murder. She was the entire family's focus for several years and I did whatever she needed me to do. My wife was found not guilty by reason of insanity and we tried to pick up the pieces of our broken lives, but I no longer valued our marriage. Given the pain I had endured, I considered myself above the rules and gradually slipped into greater and greater moral lapses.

I actually relished my leverage against God and His ways as I dared to justify my selfish lifestyle. I adopted the terse, philosophical statement of our faithless culture: *whatever.* "Whatever works for you," is the only criterion for determining truth in an unbelieving culture. So I joined the great sleeping herd of Americans mesmerized by movies, sex, techno-gadgets, and a mass media that relentlessly programs our sensual appetites. I was seeking my life, but losing it.

I was unhappily married. My vows had kept me around though my heart was long gone. I was clinically depressed—even depressed that I was depressed. I remained in this tension for seven years until finally something had to give. My wife and I separated in 1990 and later divorced.

I loved my two remaining children, stayed in their lives, and supported their mother. I began dating again, but my heart was damaged. I tried marriage a second time in 1993 but I gave up on that too. Deep down my spirit was haunted with an unsettledness that followed me and denied me any chance to start life anew with any woman. I understand now that I could not love anyone new until I had resolved my son's death and my relationship with God.

On a practical level, I replaced God the Father with my earthly father as mentor and friend. Dad had always been personable and had a good sense of humor, and even as a grown man with a career, I lived for his praise. Industriousness was the last virtue I retained and my success in an exciting career gave me self-esteem, financial security, and his approval.

I lived in my amoral limbo throughout the 1990s until I ran into a brick wall. My perfect storm began with the death of my dad on June 19, 2001. I was crushed. A few months later I pulverized my right arm in a moving accident. The injury required a bone transplant and a raft of internal hardware to make my arm functional again. The capper came three months later when I had to give up my career, due, in large part, to my own stupidity.

My life was a mess from the world's perspective and the *whatever* philosophy, which had first presented itself as egalitarian and non-judgmental, now proved completely vapid and errant. Its moral relativism had merely dulled my conscience and accommodated my baser appetites.

Whatever works only if one is safe and comfortable, but I had no more insulation by which to continue life in a spiritual holding pattern. I knew I had to stop my selfish orientation but I lacked the reason and resolve to change anything. Blaise Pascal said that two things can pierce the human heart, great beauty and great pain. I felt stripped of my securities. I was pierced with fear and desperation. I was alone and ashamed of myself. The wild *whatever* ride was done. Just sinful me with my guilt, shame, and obligations remained.

The blessing that accompanies the broken and desperate is that they know their poverty and sin. They know they must rebuild life on something real, not entertain another relativistic guess as they play out their lives. Broken people need realism and real spiritual life is based on the truth revealed to us by Jesus Christ. This is why Jesus said, "Blessed are the poor..." (Matthew 5:03). The poor in spirit know their need and can therefore embrace the truth.

Pushing the restart button was difficult. In the spring of 2002 I was forty-nine with no job and no prospects. I had two kids in school and was quickly cannibalizing my rainy–day savings. In my case the rainy day felt like a monsoon! My counselor listened and gave me an exercise. "Assess all of your options for life from two orientations. In one, embrace God in your future. In the other, consider living just as you have. Journal your reflections and let's talk next week." I did as I was asked and it was a revealing exercise. Without God, I was utterly alone and my only resource was me. Therefore I had to make life happen and duke it out with any opponent in order to survive. In this scenario, death and eternity remained dark and foreboding topics that would be best ignored or handled by distraction. Conversely, life with God would assure hope. Eternity is His business and I am His. Death would be no more.

Examining these two options, I realized I had chosen well this second time. My perfect storm had in a weird and wonderful way been worth it because my errors and resultant misfortune had awakened me to the spiritual facts of life. The simple truth is God exists and He loves me. My immediate circumstances prepared me to decide for Christ who had been waiting eighteen years since the death of my son to receive my embrace. I acknowledged my sin and failure to cooperate with Him or trust in His goodness, even when things went very, very bad. Great pain again pierced my heart, but this time for God and for good.

"What we do in life echoes through eternity" (Maximus in *Gladiator*). The line struck me like something out of the scriptures; but it came in a Hollywood script. No matter, my soul was softened up to receive wisdom whatever the source, and as plowed ground under a rain, I soaked it up. I began to make good choices like the prodigal son come to his senses. I chose to return to my Heavenly Father and I resigned myself to any life that God in His mercy might direct.

Uncertainty abounded, but there was a wild thrill at the prospect of a life completely abandoned to God. I began to listen to His still small voice during quiet mornings of prayer. I dusted off my old journal *Grey Matters*. I prayed, read scripture, and reflected. I also began to attend a Baptist church. I had no pretenses; my old life was gone. It was refreshing to take off the masks and honestly to examine my life. I walked back through the wounds, self-inflicted and otherwise, and during many restless nights

I repented my sins. During the following months my prayers brought dramatic consolation including the long–needed healing to my heart's deepest scar, my son's death.

My Baptist church pastor invited me to join a new, yearlong spiritual formation and leadership–training course that examined the sacred ground of our inner lives in order to see God's handiwork and to prepare us for service to the church. The course was the perfect complement to my professional counseling. In fact when I asked my counselor's advice on the invitation, he said, simply, "You have no choice." I cooperated and embraced the opportunity like a life preserver. The Holy Spirit led the reconstruction of my life while I met people in that course that remain dear friends to this day.

At the end of 2002, a previous client, the Association of State Employed Chaplains contacted me to work for them again. I considered the job a ministry of sorts, serving those who served the less fortunate housed in prisons and mental hospitals and the work set very well with me.

I have learned that when something resonates in my spirit, it is good to take notice. Sensitivity to certain noble themes is a sign of the Holy Spirit's message to me. Stories that move me, things I pay special attention to, things that matter to me are clues to figuring out life's next moves based on the Holy Spirit's tugging at my heartstrings. In the past, I had lived for myself, believing the lies of our consumer culture to "grab all the gusto I could get." But, gusto—what is that? It is spin for hedonism. I was sick of selfishness. Now I admired sacrifice. The stories that moved me now involved courage, sacrifice, and risk-taking on behalf of a cause larger than self. I noticed my attraction to grand sagas like J. R. R. Tolkien's *The Lord of the Rings,* historical dramas like *Band of Brothers,* or *Braveheart*, and the recollections of real-life heroes like those depicted in Tom

Brokaw's *The Greatest Generation.* That book describes our fathers, including my own, who grew up during the Great Depression and answered their country's call to risk their lives and fight against the Axis powers of World War II. I admired these real people because of the hardships they endured growing up and their young courage in a just war. It was painfully apparent I was nothing like them.

However, because such stories touched a nerve deep in my own spirit, they beckoned me to emulate them after some fashion. As I considered my own selfish life of comfort, I felt ashamed. I regretted how badly I had handled myself with my wife and family and God during the tragic time around my son's death. I could not rectify that period except to continue to do right by my former spouse (who had since remarried), and our kids. But, with new spiritual insight I could see that God was giving me another opportunity. I could respond to the call of our Savior to offer my own sacrifice according to my own capacity. The call to ministry beckoned.

Based on these inspirations and the example of the chaplains that serve the less fortunate, I decided to begin seminary studies. Looking back, it had been twenty-seven years since I first considered seminary and the ministry; now I finally followed my restored heart. There was nothing to hold me back. I was free to choose a better life, one that helped others on their spiritual journey instead of seeking my own agenda.

I began online work for a master's of divinity offered by Bethel Seminary, which serves the General Baptist Conference. I wasn't sure if I could handle seminary studies after being out of school for so long. But I was moving forward and it felt good. The online study experience served as a good trial run for me. My heart and mind thrilled at the subject matter: systematic theology, hermeneutics, church history, etc. I kept my part-time work with the chaplains and succeeded with graduate–level work. However, I noticed that all our theology derived almost exclusively from the Reformation onward. I became curious and uneasy about ignoring the previous 1,500 years of Christianity and the denomination that was today still the majority opinion of Christianity: Roman Catholicism. I began to examine honestly the "old Church" (as I called Catholicism then), and as I delved deeper into the history and development of Christian doctrine, I considered two significant questions. First, did the Church, founded by Christ's authority upon His Apostles with the guidance of the Holy Spirit, indeed survive the centuries against "the gates of hell" (Matt. 16:19) Second, had the reformers gone too far and splintered the unity of the Church by confusing her theology as they tried to reform her practice? I began an unbiased look at Catholicism for the first time in thirty years.

As I progress in my new life of faith, key events stand out in my memory to affirm God is leading my way. These events are often seen best in retrospect, though some can be discerned immediately because they are so vivid. Such milestones are ignored only at my peril and one of my first ones came like a bolt from the blue. While driving along the stunning central coast of California on June 19, 2003, as a result of a small sign and a strong, spontaneous impulse, I deliberately detoured off Highway 1 and turned up a side road. After winding up 1,000 feet of mountainside I came upon a Benedictine monastery, New Camaldoli Hermitage. I had no clue what I was doing but the view was spectacular! The date was coincidently the anniversary of my father's passing. As I discussed this odd convergence with the date and my off-road impulse the monk in the bookstore amazed me when he revealed that it was also the anniversary of *their* father's passing (St.

Romuald the founder of the Camaldolese Benedictines). Then he stated impishly, "I think our fathers have been talking." I agreed and immediately booked a retreat.

At the monastery I was introduced to the ancient discipline of the Divine Office and found its regular rhythm of fixed prayers from the Psalms and scriptures and ancient homilies to be a formative spiritual exercise. I was just restarting my faith journey with the assistance of the good Baptists, but I returned to my New Camaldoli haven every six months for the next three years. My eventual return to the fullness of the Faith began in August 2005 when I was allowed to become an oblate with the Camaldolese—a lay person who promises to observe the Divine Office. That same year I began to read from my Divine Office breviary at my Baptist men's weekly breakfast and I also led my group to the monastery. One of the men actually preceded my return to the Church!

Another milestone came in November 2005 when I took my mother on a pilgrimage to Venice, Assisi, and Rome. The trip went flawlessly for seventeen days as we visited the great churches and sites of Christian culture and spirituality. There the beauty of the Lord and the seamless history of His Church seduced me. I saw the final resting place of Christ's chief apostle St. Peter, and the great missionary St. Paul, both buried in Rome. I was amazed to learn that there has been an unbroken line of bishops of Rome since St. Peter's reign, and that his bones were successfully excavated and confirmed underneath St. Peter's basilica in the 1940s. Then, on a misty weekday at St. Paul's-Beyond-the-Walls, when I was all alone inside the nave sitting on a bench looking up at a great mosaic of Christ in the apse behind the main altar, I got the inspiration that my call to the ministry would be not in a protestant denomination, but in the Catholic

Church. This was a thought that I had never entertained before, but given my affinity for New Camaldoli I no longer felt any prejudice toward things Catholic. As I sat praying and pondering how I might confirm such a leading, the sun broke through the clouds and shone through the clerestory windows, illuminating my seat in a small, brilliant circle. It was as if God were dramatically confirming the call. It also seemed like a Hollywood cliché. So I chalked up the sunbeam as a coincidence, and as it faded away, I reasoned that if the Holy Spirit was truly behind the guidance and the sudden sunshine some other confirmation would follow. Seconds later, right on cue, the light show repeated itself. As I basked in the light a second time I recorded the milestone in my journal.

On my return from the pilgrimage I discontinued my studies with Bethel and a year later transferred my theological studies to a Catholic university. This time I selected a Jesuit institution, Seattle University, based largely on its location. I downsized my life, sold my condo in Sacramento, CA, part of what I termed "Operation Pearl of Great Price," and began moving my life to Seattle. However, I canceled my plans when my mother was diagnosed with pancreatic cancer in the summer of 2006. As the only unmarried son out of four brothers, I felt it incumbent on me to attend to her. Instead, I moved to Mom's little cottage and to the very same parish I had been baptized in fifty-three years earlier, Our Lady of Angels Catholic Church, in Hermiston, Oregon.

The decision to spend time serving Mom was the best decision I had made in a long time. My return to the Catholic Church was an answer to Mom's prayers during the many years I had wandered. She received back the care I had received from her when I was a child. I cooked, cleaned, ran her to the doctor, and together we prayed the Divine Office twice a day. I served at daily Mass at Our Lady of Angels, which was only three blocks from her home. On July 9, 2007, my mother died peacefully.

Was my interest in the priesthood my own wishful thinking? I had entertained illusions before that presumed upon God's will. But Mom's old friends in the parish often innocently and unintentionally guided my discernment and sharpened my desire to become a priest. Often people say others' observations give a more objective view because they can see our blind spots for us. Devout parishioners now challenged me to consider the priesthood, and their efforts reinforced what I had experienced during the Rome pilgrimage. The call got stronger.

Oddly, marriage still seemed a possibility for me. At fifty-four, I was in decent shape, healthy, and with a normal libido. But I was not pursuing marriage or any woman. I had girlfriends, but I was only interested in platonic friendships. I thought about the sacrifice a priest makes by promising to observe the evangelical counsels: poverty, chastity and obedience. Compared to the protestant track for ministry this was extremely radical stuff.

What American male seeks such a life? What could motivate a man to choose freely such a countercultural life? Only the love of God can fuel such a sacrifice. What would it look like to be single–heartedly committed to Him? Did I want a greater spiritual intimacy with Christ than I had at present? More to the point, could Christ's love be so big that a man could be satisfied with Him and not a woman? Would He reveal more of Himself and His love for me as I moved closer to Him? I figured that I had to pursue my sense of call seriously because if I did not, I would regret my reluctance until the day I died and perhaps for eternity! I resolved to begin the process again.

My previous marriages loomed as obstacles to the

priesthood. I began by speaking with my pastor, Fr. Peter Auer, SOLT, who helped me submit the proper forms to our diocese for consideration. I had not been married in the Catholic Church and due to "lack of form" I was issued Certificates of Freedom in short order. When he received these documents, Fr. Peter called me into his parish office and said enthusiastically, "Here, Skip, now you can be a priest"! I was shocked by his comment, but looking back, I sense he may have been prophetic.

In my own heart and mind I was in a good spiritual place with God and significant healing had taken place in the years since 2002. Given my new freedom, if ever a time had come for me to court a wife, it was now. Everything was in order. I even owned a home free and clear. But God's inspired word advises, "It is good for a man not to marry. . . . I would like you to be free from concern. An unmarried man is concerned about the Lord's affairs—how he can please the Lord." (1 Cor. 7:1, 32) I took this advice to heart and relaxed with the idea that God might be calling me to be a priest.

I think men's hearts are designed to embrace the extraordinary—wild things that call us outside ourselves. A daring sense of sacrifice for something holy and good to be embraced only when we relinquish our desires can be exhilarating. Submission to God's prompting satisfies some deep design in our spirit. As I began to understand myself, the call to the priesthood became clearer and my spirit responded with a quiet and growing *yes*. Thoughts of being a priest did not fill me with dread of some insurmountable ascetical burden. The thought set well with me. I reflected on Phil. 2:13, "for it is God who works in you to will and to act according to his good purpose." I thrilled to a sense of abandonment to God's purposes and a larger life work than satisfying my own pleasure. The idea was pleasurable nonetheless, but in a purer way. To serve Christ's Church directly as a priest is a work that demands my life. It is a higher call to fatherhood, one with a holy and eternal nature.

I began my first steps in pursuit of this vocation with my home diocese of Baker, Oregon. After a brief discussion with the vocation director I was judged too old. As I continued to make inquiries and was turned away, again and again, I discovered two things. First, mature age, and by that I mean over forty-five, is a disadvantage. Many dioceses and orders view entrance to their ranks from an economic cost benefit analysis and whether their investment of time and money can pay. I can understand this thinking and sympathize with it.

Additionally, there is the human formation problem: older men just don't mold as easily as younger men. It is easier to train the tree when the wood is young than after it is old and stiff.

Secondly, the infallible Church is a collection of fallible human beings. Many laity and some religious societies or orders and even some bishops disagree with the authoritative Magisterium and have a democratic view of the Church. They seek to change her from within as though she were just another organization. Their formula may work for government or corporations, and the model exists in almost all protestant churches, but it is not the way Christ established Israel or His Church. It is not the way the Roman Catholic Church operates. The sheep don't vote for the shepherd. While investigating various groups and dioceses, I encountered unorthodox and liberal factions and quickly dismissed them from consideration. If my age did not disqualify me in the first place, I disqualified them.

Over time I approached seven Catholic orders in a row and was shot down by each. Even if some had said yes to me, I would have declined because I was done with Protestantism and the liberalism that protests Christ's Church from without and within. I wanted to learn from priests and doctors who would teach what the Church taught. I reflected on whether this string of denials was the perfect "no" to my discernment effort, or if I might be on the edge of success and needed to persevere. One thing was sure; the devil no longer had me. Not only was I back in the Church, but I was lining up to serve in a consecrated life. Yes, he was working against me. But I still had one more card to play.

I first learned of Holy Apostles Seminary from my pastor at Our Lady of Angels Fr. Peter Auer, SOLT, who recommended it because of its fidelity to the Magisterium. The two priests who succeeded Fr. Auer, Fr. Mike Hinken, SOLT and Fr. Andrew Szymakowski, FSSP, also supported my orientation toward Holy Apostles. The question was: how to get there? You do not just apply directly to a major Catholic seminary as to a graduate school or a protestant seminary. A diocese or an order must sponsor you.

I needed to talk to someone. So, I called and spoke to a priest from the Missionaries of the Holy Apostles, the society that founded the seminary in 1957. Fr. Bradley Pierce, MSA and I got the age issue out of the way quickly. "Oh, fifty-four? That's fine, no problem. Our charism is to invite and accompany mature men for the priesthood. However, we start drawing the line at fifty-five," he stated matter-of-factly. Those words were music to my ears. When I clarified that my interest in Holy Apostles was based on its fidelity to the Magisterium he perked up. He wanted to learn a little more about me and I took a breath and described the good, the bad, and the ugly. After a heart-to-heart discussion with Fr. Brad and with his warm encouragement, I made arrangements to visit Holy Apostles Seminary in the summer of 2008. After a frank discussion with the provincial, Fr. Tad Hallock, MSA, the society accepted me and offered a postulancy. The rector, Fr. Doug Mosey reviewed my application and granted formal acceptance. I was set to begin formation in January 2009. I was elated!

I arrived at Holy Apostles with the determination that, no matter what, I would love the experience. And I have. I see my life with the Missionaries of the Holy Apostles as the opportunity of a lifetime. I have lived several lives by now, and to compare—this is wild! I am not about to lose sight of the fact that the Lord led me here and opened the door. "Operation Pearl of Great Price" has worked and by selling everything, with the Lord's help, I have resources to pay for my studies. The Missionaries of the Holy Apostles were the only society that gave me, a late-vocation hopeful, a chance. The Holy Spirit has truly been at work.

One of my favorite parables is from Matt. 20:1-16. It describes the generous heart of God, the vineyard owner, and the late workers. Jesus tells the story of some men who were ignored all day in the marketplace and near the end they had been fruitless. Wonderfully, the vineyard owner hires them saying, "You also go and work in my vineyard." The lesson is that Our Lord redeems our opportunities no matter what time of life if we will let Him. All of our mileposts point to His handiwork. I am anxious to see how this journey continues and most importantly, who will join me in the vineyard!

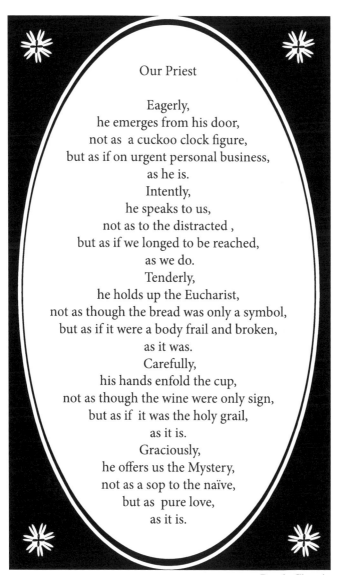

Our Priest

Eagerly,
he emerges from his door,
not as a cuckoo clock figure,
but as if on urgent personal business,
as he is.
Intently,
he speaks to us,
not as to the distracted ,
but as if we longed to be reached,
as we do.
Tenderly,
he holds up the Eucharist,
not as though the bread was only a symbol,
but as if it were a body frail and broken,
as it was.
Carefully,
his hands enfold the cup,
not as though the wine were only sign,
but as if it was the holy grail,
as it is.
Graciously,
he offers us the Mystery,
not as a sop to the naïve,
but as pure love,
as it is.

Ronda Chervin

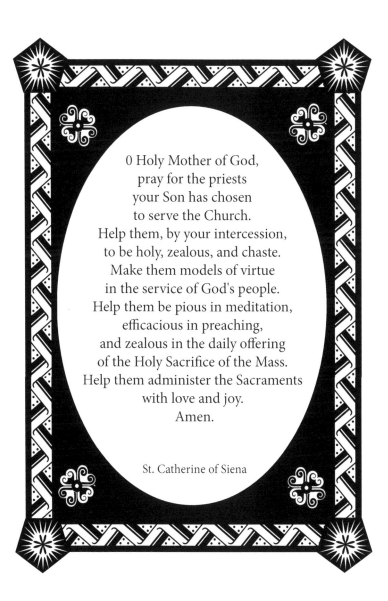

0 Holy Mother of God,
pray for the priests
your Son has chosen
to serve the Church.
Help them, by your intercession,
to be holy, zealous, and chaste.
Make them models of virtue
in the service of God's people.
Help them be pious in meditation,
efficacious in preaching,
and zealous in the daily offering
of the Holy Sacrifice of the Mass.
Help them administer the Sacraments
with love and joy.
Amen.

St. Catherine of Siena

Simple Call for a Great Mission

Rev. Luis Luna, M.S.A.

Allowing ourselves to let go of anger and forgive are the hallmarks of this story. Childhood grievances toward parents, even siblings, can linger and taint a relationship with God if we don't act on God's g0race to reconcile. Fr. Luna also touches significantly on the common claim of those who give their lives for others: "They evangelize me."

My name is Father Luis Antonio Luna Barrera. I was born in 1958 in the province of Lima, Peru, in the middle of the Andes, in the town of Gorgor. I was the fifth of ten children.

My mother was a widow with four children when I was conceived outof wedlock. Her family was well educated and included teachers, soldiers and engineers. My father's family was largely made up of farmers.

It is a tradition in Peruvian families that one of the children lives with his grandmother, so I lived with my blind grandmother until I was ten years old, when she passed away. It was during this time that my dad married my mom and formed a family. I felt anger about this situation, and found it difficult to adjust to this new life. It affected my relationship with my father for five years. My father was reserved, never affectionate. He would show love by doing things for me, which I only understood later. Only Our Lord Jesus helped me to understand and forgive my parents, especially my dad. No one else helped.

I took part in the family work of making cheese and putting it into containers to sell to people. We also had land in the mountains which we let to others to farm.

The prayer life of my town was in the hands of a good, unmarried woman who had the keys to the church, which she opened on Saturday for the Rosary. There were no regular Sunday Masses. The big religious holidays occurred two times a year: December 8, the Feast of the Immaculate Conception, and Holy Week. Since I had been baptized on December 8, this was a very important day to me. From my early years I loved to go to the church, and I learned to sing and pray with my grandmother. I was close to the missionaries when they visited my town.

There was an elementary school in our town with forty-five children in each class. I was the third youngest in the class—some were in their teens because they had dropped out to work during school times. The student to finish first in the class received a scholarship to high school, and since we were not rich, that was essential for me. I managed to become that first–ranked student and go to high school in Lima.

I went to study at Our Lady of Guadalupe High School, which was rated the best in the nation. I lived with my uncle and cousins on my father's side. It was a huge challenge because of the deteriorating relationship with my dad, and I did stupid things like smoking and drinking just to displease him and hurt him. I knew it was wrong. In my first ten years I had experienced so much joy in my mother's family, but my father's relatives justified my behavior as good. They were wrong, and I was not happy.

During high school I never went back to see my parents. My mom would come to Lima to see me instead. My dad's family, not very religious, went to Mass twice a year, even though there was a church two blocks from the house. The young men in the family thought church was for women.

One night when I was seventeen I got tired of being unhappy. At school, a priest gave me a Bible and said, "Luna, when you don't see a meaning in your life, open the Bible and you will find it." That night I was so empty, and I thought, I want a solution. So, I opened the Bible and found this passage, Revelation 3:20: "Here I stand, knocking at the door. If anyone hears me calling and opens the door, I will enter his house and have supper with him, and he with me."

I said to God: I have been looking for a long time, such a

That same night I made a deal with God. If you do that for me, I will become a priest. He answered immediately. The next day I looked out of the window and the world looked different. The flowers and birds looked beautiful. I said "Good morning" to my relatives. Everyone was surprised. I thanked my aunt and cleaned the dishes. After three days my uncle asked if I was sick. I answered, "No, I was sick. This is the real me." My room, which I could lock, was the place my friends and I had stored liquor. I cleaned it, and the next day, after my experience with Jesus, I had the others take all the liquor away. I started going to church. I didn't care what anyone thought. Usually, I prayed only with the women.

Then, I thought, What am I missing? God, let me know. God replied, Talk to your dad.

My uncle first told me not to go, but then said he would go with me. But I told him I needed to go alone.

I arrived at our little town. My mom was shocked. I hadn't been back for five years! She wanted to go with me to find my dad on the land, but I said I needed to go alone, and I promised her it would be okay. When my dad saw me, he watched until we came eye to eye.

"Dad, it's time to talk," I said. "Yes, it's time," he agreed.

Now, as a man, I understood his motives better. I apologized for being so rough. We hugged and let many tears come down, but we were totally reconciled. After that I never had a single bad word with him.

One year later, when I was finishing high school, I went to see the Franciscans, because I needed to pay my Lord for all the good things He had done for me. The priest asked me how I liked parish life. He could see I didn't have a vocation with them but said to come back the following year.

I was so happy for his answer, because I had kept my promise, and now I was off the hook. I said to Jesus, See, I did what I said. Now I am going back to Gorgor, and You have to come get me there if You want me.

I went back to the town to prepare for the university exam which was very tough, because there were so many applicants for so few places! I spent one year preparing, and I won my place. My father was very happy and he sold some bulls to pay for my tuition. He wanted me to be a professional man, which was good because I had always liked school more than farming. Now I had taken the examination and succeeded.

The whole year no priest came to my town. I was ready to go back to Lima, but inside of me was different. I was waiting always for a priest. Every time I saw a strange car I thought it might be bringing a priest, sent by Jesus to get me. In the meantime, my spiritual life was growing. I prayed a great deal; I learned church music. My friends accepted my new form of life. They were always in the cantinas, and I was always in the church with the Legion of Mary praying in the evening.

I planned to go to the University in January, but on December 8, 1978, a priest came on a horse! My friends and I were on our way to play soccer for the championship when the priest singled me out and said to leave the game and come with him. He kept finding reasons to keep me, and we spent the whole day together. I was terrified that this was the last call that I had been waiting for, and there was no escape! He was sleeping at the house of my aunt.

Finally he asked, "Do you want to become a priest?"

I said, "What, you want me to be a church mouse?"

The priest, who turned out to be Fr. David Zercie of the Missionaries of the Holy Apostles, told me that he was in another town and the Holy Spirit pushed him to come here to my town because there was a vocation. "When I saw you, Luis, I thought it was you."

"Okay," I said, and told him my whole story. Fr. Zercie said he would recommend me.

"When are you returning to Lima?" I asked.

Then I told Mama, but she didn't understand. I told her I would be a good priest and help others with the same problems in their families as we had. She kissed me and said, "Now you need to convince your dad."

My dad said, "I sold the bulls. You should go to the University." "Dad, I want to try," I told him. He answered, "If you go to be a priest, that is serious because with God you don't play." When my dad realized that I was serious, he prayed the Rosary every day for me.

Even though I did not yet have my papers from the high school, Fr. Maximo, the rector at the Seminary of the Holy Apostles in Lima, accepted me. This seminary was founded in 1962. In Peru at that time, most boys would go to the minor seminary at the ages of seven to twelve. This made me, at nineteen, a late vocation!

Fr. Maximo told me to come back January 1. This was

1979. The first weeks were difficult because I was used to staying up with friends, sometimes until 2 a.m., and here we went to bed at 10 p.m. I thought, I can't stand this boring place, but I'll stay a week. And so it went—a week, then another week. I loved the studies and was a good student.

So, I promised Jesus to live only for Him. If I wanted a different lifestyle, I would quit. I would strive to be a good priest. And now, at age fifty-two I am still trying to be faithful to this commitment.

In the course of the years, I studied, first, philosophy in Lima. After that I went to Rome, to the Gregorian University, and finally to Ottawa, Canada, for canon law. I made my definitive promises in the society of apostolic life, the Missionaries of the Holy Apostles, in August 1985; I was ordained a priest on January 18, 1987.

I have served in many countries, including the jungles of Colombia, and in priestly formation in Peru where I was eventually rector. I was the superior in Venezuela and also a canon lawyer for the Diocese of Los Tequetes. I was also part of the administration of the student house in Ottawa. In 1999 I came to the United States to teach at Holy Apostles College and Seminary in Cromwell, Connecticut, where I now live. I love best to teach and form future priests and lay people in the service of the Church.

Working in this extraordinary mission, in the name of the Lord, has given me many satisfactions. Surely I don't merit it. It is only for the glory of God that He showed His love for this little and unworthy priest. I have been able to build a church in my hometown and have preached missions there. I was even able to hear my father's confession and give him the anointing of the sick. In a place where there were very few priests, two of my relatives became priests. At my dad's funeral there were fifty priests!

I would like to give just a few highlights of my life as a priest. When I left Rome, I went to the jungle of Colombia as a missionary. I had to walk through the jungle, sometimes without food, with broken shoes. The relationship with other priests was not always easy because of my temperament, but this helped me come to my second conversion: to suffer for Jesus without complaints, trying to do only what is commanded, trying to see what Jesus is teaching me in hard times. I try to be open. I pray, I know You love me, and if You permit this, You have a reason. I am sure You will always protect me. Now, I surrender. Later, I will understand.

I learned to see in the eyes of the poor the presence of Jesus, and I became sensitive to their sufferings, while sharing their destiny. But I think I did poorly. It was always they who evangelized me. For example, for some time as a young priest I was chaplain of the contemplative nuns. My task was to say the Mass at 7:30 a.m. From my seminary to their house was a distance of several blocks, so I ran fast every day. In that place were so many poor homeless people. One day I saw one of them dead, but I was late, so I crossed to the other side of the street and continued on my way. I wanted to be on time. As I was entering in the Church, I stopped with tears in my eyes because I felt miserable. I had abandoned Jesus in the person of the homeless man, and I was unable to celebrate the Mass. So I went back. To my surprise, the people told me, "Thank you, Father, that you came back." So I prayed for him. I meditated on the Word of God, and that was my homily later. The lesson was hard. I believe He always teaches me like that because I'm the slowest of His students. Still, He loves me.

During the time of violence in Peru it was hard to go to missions, because everyone could be in danger; many of my relatives were killed. One time during Mass, these violent men came and were listening to me. Some priests had already been killed. I was scared, but I thought, I won't run away. I will just say this Mass as my last. I saw the men sitting in a pew with guns trained on me, but I received the grace to give a good homily and finish the Mass. They walked out. Even though they were trained to kill all priests, they found me sincere and they couldn't shoot!

I cannot write all the wonders that God has done using this poor instrument. I have learned that with every act of my daily life, if I listen to Him and obey Him, He will make miracles. Now I am no longer surprised, because He loves His ministers to be his instruments. I try to be all the more docile in His hands. Sometimes I have success, but many, many other times I don't surrender totally to His will. He asks all, and I am not always ready to give myself totally. I am still working at it, so if you read this, pray for me.

Here is my final thought about my life: If God gave me another life on earth and allowed me to choose, I am sure I would choose again to be a priest. Not because I am a great priest, but because He is wonderful, and can make good things happen using unusual vessels like me. I'm so happy when I hear expressions like, "This is Luis? I can't believe he is a priest!" Thank you, God, for Your love, mercy, and generosity toward me. How can I repay God for the good He has done for me? I will lift up the cup of salvation and invoke His name forever!

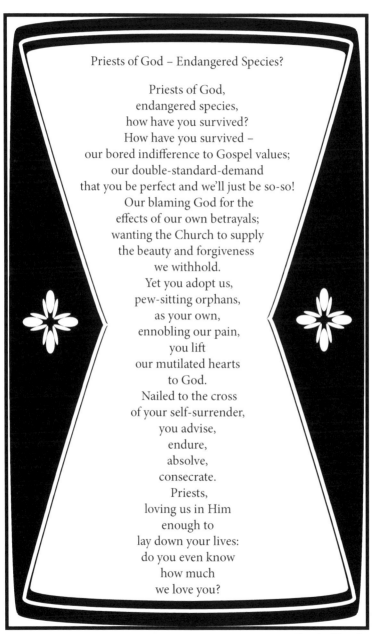

Priests of God – Endangered Species?

Priests of God,
endangered species,
how have you survived?
How have you survived –
our bored indifference to Gospel values;
our double-standard-demand
that you be perfect and we'll just be so-so!
Our blaming God for the
effects of our own betrayals;
wanting the Church to supply
the beauty and forgiveness
we withhold.
Yet you adopt us,
pew-sitting orphans,
as your own,
ennobling our pain,
you lift
our mutilated hearts
to God.
Nailed to the cross
of your self-surrender,
you advise,
endure,
absolve,
consecrate.
Priests,
loving us in Him
enough to
lay down your lives:
do you even know
how much
we love you?

Ronda Chervin

53

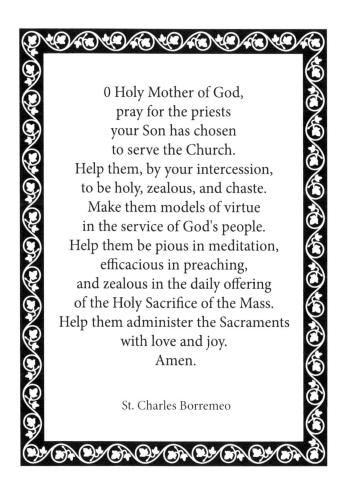

0 Holy Mother of God,
pray for the priests
your Son has chosen
to serve the Church.
Help them, by your intercession,
to be holy, zealous, and chaste.
Make them models of virtue
in the service of God's people.
Help them be pious in meditation,
efficacious in preaching,
and zealous in the daily offering
of the Holy Sacrifice of the Mass.
Help them administer the Sacraments
with love and joy.
Amen.

St. Charles Borremeo

Is God Telling You Something?

Rev. Deacon John B. Trambley, II

Fr. Trambley tells of the quiet heroism of ordinary people such as his parents and grandmother, who in their faithfulness serve as powerful examples of the way we should live. His response to the personal invitation of his archbishop is also instructive.

I was born on May 17, 1966, in Ames, Iowa. Back then, Dad was working on his Ph.D. in higher education administration at Iowa State University and Mom was a third grade teacher at Meeker Elementary School. My sister Jennifer was born April 8, 1968. That ended Mom's teaching career! She decided to devote her time and energies to raising us.

Growing up in Iowa, I never thought about leaving the Catholic Church. I knew about the existence of other faith traditions, but I was happy to remain Catholic. I remember the night I agreed to serve as an altar boy at St. Mary of Nazareth Catholic Church. I had a feeling of peace that I had not experienced before. I think it was my first indication that I had a vocation to priestly ministry.

After Dad earned his doctorate, we moved to Clarinda, Iowa, where he became the dean and director of the Clarinda campus of Iowa Western Community College.

I attended kindergarten there and remember playing in the backyard of our home. We had lived in a trailer in Ames, but this first real house had nice green grass.

When it became obvious that there was a plan to close the campus in Clarinda, Dad quit his job to protest the policies of his boss. This led to some stories in the media. There were government hearings and they resulted in keeping the college where it was. Dad had sacrificed his job for the good of the community. I've always been a little bit in awe about that. To this day, Iowa Western Community College is doing very well in Clarinda. I think his example of sacrifice prepared me to understand the meaning of Christ's sacrificial love for His Church.

Dad couldn't find another job as a dean after this controversy, so he changed careers. He was hired by Management Recruiters, Inc. and moved all of us to Des Moines. Eventually, he opened his own recruiting business called The Recruiter, Inc. He remained self-employed for thirty years until he retired in 2003. He had a table in the basement which served as his home office when he wasn't at work, and I have many memories of his making phone calls at night.

I joined the Boy Scouts of America, and with the help and encouragement of my parents, earned both the Eagle Scout and Ad Altare Dei awards. My service project to earn the rank of Eagle Scout was to lead a group of scouts in repainting a fence at Living History Farms on the edge of Des Moines, Iowa. The visiting tourists got a chuckle out of all of us. We looked like a scene from The Adventures of Huckleberry Finn. A short time later, in 1979, Pope John Paul II visited Iowa and he celebrated Mass at Living History Farms in front of 250,000 people. We joked that he was coming to inspect the paint job. My grandmother, my parents, and my sister and I all made the pilgrimage on foot to take part in the Mass since no cars were allowed. It was the first time I had ever seen the Pope.

As members of St. Mary of Nazareth Catholic Church in Des Moines, our family interpreted "full and active participation" as meaning we should all be doing something. Dad served as a lector and also on the parish council. My sister played guitar at Sunday Mass, and I served as altar boy or lector. Mom was the one who supported us as she prayed in the pews.

I enjoyed the CCD classes, but there were times when I clashed with some of the other students in my class. I was the skinny, shy kid, and often the target of teasing. When the religious sister wasn't looking, some of the kids would throw spitballs at me. After complaining about this to my father, he made a suggestion. He said the next time it happens, just say "Ouch!" as loud as possible, then stand up and say, "Sister, these fine young Christians hit me with a spitball!" Well, the next week I returned to class. Sure enough, I saw that they were preparing to throw another spitball at me. I waited and pretended not to notice. I was ready. As soon as they got the chance, I was hit!

I delivered on cue: "Ouch!" and the room immediately fell silent. I stood up, turned toward our teacher and said, "Sister, these fine young Christians hit me with a spitball!" Sister marched the perpetrators out of the room and read them the riot act. I have had a very favorable impression of religious ever since! I also discovered that I loved performing!

My activities in high school included choir, drama and swing choir. My sister and I both auditioned for high school plays and musicals and we both continued to participate in theater in college. Once, in high school, we performed together as husband and wife in a comedy called Lily, the Felon's Daughter. My role was Jonas. I enjoyed making the audience laugh.

I really liked being in swing choir in high school as well. We would hire a choreographer to create our song and dance routines before we went to state competition. Those were fun. We often got out of class to perform at local nursing homes and retirement homes too. When you are in high school, you feel very important every time you get a pass to get out of class.

We also went on family vacations at least a couple of times a year. One of our holidays each year was to go skiing and the other was to tour places of historical significance. I enjoyed both kinds of trips, but I grew to love our ski trips to Colorado. Skiing was a sport I could do, and it didn't matter that I wasn't especially tall or strong. It was peaceful. It was like being a little closer to God. You could see for miles when you reached the top of the lift. I also enjoyed the many conversations I had with Dad as we rode the chair lift.

Starting in 1984, I spent four summers on the seasonal staff of Philmont Scout Ranch in Cimarron, New Mexico. I sent in my application with the encouragement of another scout and the camp accepted me to work in the food services area. I was a little disappointed that I didn't get a good assignment, but I accepted it. I spent the summer washing dishes, serving food, and cleaning the dining hall. The next year I applied again and I finally got what I wanted, which was to work in the backcountry. The first summer in the backcountry I taught fly-fishing. By the next summer I was teaching roping, branding and horseback riding. The last summer I taught blacksmithing and gold panning, and gave tours of an old gold mine. Those were some of the best days of my life.

During my college years, I studied art and mass communication at Buena Vista University in Iowa. The school had a new mass communications building which gave all of the students a chance to use the latest equipment. I was a disc jockey, a reporter for the student newspaper, a producer for the television station, and I also studied studio art. I didn't have much time off!

In 1988 I took a class trip to Europe. It was focused on studying European art, but we took the time to see other things as well. On Wednesday, January 13, I was able to join the audience in Rome to see Pope John Paul II for the second time. His message was to have faith because Jesus is raised from the dead!

Meanwhile, my parents had been looking for a new place to live because they were tired of Iowa's heat and humidity during the summer and snow in the winter. Snow is no fun if you can't ski on it! So, in 1988, they moved to Albuquerque, New Mexico, along with my dad's mom and one of his sisters.

When I graduated from Buena Vista University in 1989, I moved to New Mexico to be closer to my parents, aunt, and grandmother. I didn't have a job yet, so my idea was to spend a couple of weeks resting and updating my resume. Dad had other plans. He told me to start knocking on doors and meeting people. It worked and I soon had a job. I also attended St. Bernadette's Catholic Church where a parishioner asked me if I had ever thought about being a priest. I said I was planning to be an artist or work in television.

My work kept me busy and I would sometimes join my parents for Mass on Sunday, or I would often drive my grandmother to Mass at Our Lady of Fatima. Even though I had not registered in a parish, I felt I belonged and never missed Mass.

I drove my grandmother to Sunday Mass at Our Lady of Fatima until she was placed in hospice care. She died in 1993 of cancer. Her death was a shock to all of us. I was glad to get to know her in the few years she spent with us because when she lived in North Dakota I had only visited a couple of times growing up. My grandmother showed great courage and faith through the final stages of her battle with cancer. She was a faithful Catholic her entire life, often praying the Rosary and leaving a lasting impression of her faith on me.

After working briefly as a graphic artist, I was hired full-time by KOAT-TV where I spent almost fifteen years working in the programming department. I started as a programming and mail-room assistant. I delivered packages, edited nudity and adult language out of movies before they aired and checked and labeled other shows and placed them into the run for the master-control operators. Sometimes, during an election, I would help the people in the news department by counting the returns—and eating their pizza!

When I was dubbing or editing movies, I usually did the second reel of the movie first and then the first reel second. In this way, I avoided spending my time at work "watching television". That scruple was kind of silly. Of course I was supposed to watch TV at work! I had such a complex about mixing work and pleasure. In my world, work and pleasure did not mix. Work is work. Pleasure is pleasure. You didn't date people from work, because it makes work more difficult if you break up with a coworker. I guess I felt that I needed to stay focused on my job while at work. Now I'm starting to see how I remained single all these years!

Actually, I did date, but none of the women I dated seemed like "the one". I also listened very carefully to what my dates said. If they said they didn't want children, I took that seriously. I knew that if I were married, I wanted to have a family. I even dated one person for several years but I never felt like the relationship was progressing in the right direction. I thought I might be too particular, but I wanted to find someone who shared my views and wasn't a messy housekeeper. I am a horrible housekeeper, so I knew marrying a messy person would mean we would be buried alive in junk!

When the assistant program director quit, I was promoted to that position. I had expanded paperwork in addition to my previous responsibilities. Then, when the program director retired in 2000, I took over. It was a good job with a decent salary and benefits and it came with many responsibilities. I was able to meet and go to lunch with sales representatives from major syndicators of television programming. I had my own business cards and my own office. Still, I felt like the job wasn't right for me. I was also working many additional hours every week. My days stretched from 8:00a.m. to 8:00p.m.—hardly a forty-hour week.

Thanks to my father's insistence that our family take time for skiing, we still went to Colorado for ski trips on a regular basis. It was good stress relief and a chance to gain some perspective on things. We found a nice Catholic church in Pagosa Springs, Colorado, with a friendly pastor who also played the organ.

For a long time, I didn't understand the True Presence of Christ in the holy Eucharist. It wasn't until I went on one of these vacations to Pagosa Springs, and heard a former protestant minister preaching a mission that I realized the True Presence was real. It was not just a symbol. This realization made all of the difference in my faith journey. Suddenly, the prayers of the Holy Sacrifice of the Mass made sense. Eucharistic Adoration made sense. As "The Credo of the People of God" says, "The bread and wine consecrated by the priest are changed into the body and blood of Christ enthroned gloriously in heaven, and we believe that the mysterious presence of the Lord, under what continues to appear to our senses as before, is a true, real and substantial presence" (proclaimed by Pope Paul VI, June 30, 1968). Thanks to the witness of this former protestant minister, my faith deepened in one night.

I moved to a new part of town and started attending Risen Savior Catholic Community. The new pastor, who arrived in 2000, asked me to consider being a priest. At first I didn't do anything because I still felt my calling was to a career in television. However, I never felt completely at peace. There would be days filled with angry callers, piles of paperwork, and missed feeds. When I got home every night I often wondered if it was all worth it. Money was never something I cared about very much. Yes, I knew it was necessary to pay bills, but I wasn't motivated by money. Instead, I was haunted by something one of my art professors had told me in college. "Making money is easy. What is difficult is doing good work." Now, I realize that he was talking about art, but it applies to other areas as well. Jesus said, "You cannot serve God and mammon." (Matt. 6:24) I was starting to feel that I was meant for more than working as a program director at an ABC affiliate in Albuquerque for the rest of my life.

In 2001, I started attending Theology on Tap, a monthly gathering of Catholic adults. The purpose was to learn something about the Catholic faith and enjoy food and fellowship as well. Well, at one meeting of Theology on Tap, I heard a speaker say that if you are not at peace, that could be God telling you something. I felt those words were directed at me!

Once during a particularly rough day at the office, I started looking around the internet for information about vocations to the priesthood and religious life. I found out there was an upcoming vocation discernment weekend sponsored by the Archdiocese of Santa Fe. I printed the sign-up form and thought seriously about going, but I was afraid to go. I didn't submit the forms. The next year, I also printed the form for the vocation discernment weekend. I thought I would go, but then I decided I wasn't worthy and didn't send it in. I remember my sister asking if I had decided to go and then telling her no. Well, the next year I was having a really bad day at the office and I printed the form for the vocation discernment weekend one more time. I even filled it out, but then I started having second thoughts about going. I asked my dad about it. He gave me some valuable advice. He said, "Just go to the weekend. Either there will be something there for you or there won't be something there for you, but either way you will stop talking about it!" I finally sent the application in 2005.

Once I arrived at the weekend, I was welcomed warmly. I heard the vocation stories of several priests. I learned how priests lift people up and make space for God at the most important moments in life. I also had the opportunity to sit down with Archbishop Michael J. Sheehan for an interview. I was quite nervous about that! My palms were sweaty. He immediately put me at ease and we had a nice long chat. At the end of the interview, he told me he didn't see anything that would hinder me from being a priest. I left the weekend filled with excitement that this might be a real possibility for me. I didn't commit right away. I wanted to think about it, but both the archbishop and the vocation director made follow-up calls, encouraging me to consider seriously a vocation to the priesthood.

A few weeks later, I joined Archbishop Sheehan in the pilgrimage to Chimayo on Good Friday. Thousands of Catholics walked together. After the pilgrimage we ate lunch, and during that break he told me he still thought I had a vocation to be a priest. I didn't say anything. Finally, on the drive to the Santa Fe County Correctional Facility to pray the Stations of the Cross with the inmates, he asked if I was going to do this or not. I told him I thought I was ready to take this direction as far as it would lead. I entered seminary that same year with the goal of discerning how I could best serve. Now, after several years of study, I have received a letter from Archbishop Sheehan calling me to the priesthood. (Note from Dr. Ronda Chervin: The ordination took place on June 26, 2010.)

I feel now that this is what I have been preparing for my whole life. Priesthood simply builds upon the experiences I have lived through and the things I have learned. Everything I have done was necessary to get me to this point. I needed to try different things, such as working in a television station. I needed to spend time away from school to figure out what direction my life should take. I often prayed for a sign, wondering why my life didn't feel like it was going anywhere. Now, I finally feel that my life has purpose. In choosing to do God's will for me, I have found the peace and contentment that I lacked when I pursued my own will. God is very merciful indeed.

Mary's Beloved Priest

By motherly love held secure,
your heart
is worn on your sleeve.

Overshadowed by the Holy Spirit,
your fervor
glows without restraint.

Taught by one whose love knows no limit,
your caring
passes no-one by.

Closen to be Christ again to the world,
your feet
can never flee the cross.

Attached by beads to a glorified Queen,
your hope
is boundless!

Ronda Chervin

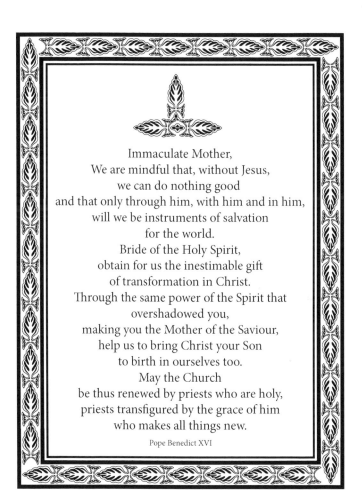

Immaculate Mother,
We are mindful that, without Jesus,
we can do nothing good
and that only through him, with him and in him,
will we be instruments of salvation
for the world.
Bride of the Holy Spirit,
obtain for us the inestimable gift
of transformation in Christ.
Through the same power of the Spirit that
overshadowed you,
making you the Mother of the Saviour,
help us to bring Christ your Son
to birth in ourselves too.
May the Church
be thus renewed by priests who are holy,
priests transfigured by the grace of him
who makes all things new.

Pope Benedict XVI

Only God Can Change Me

Youssef-Mariam Hanna, CFR

God may speak to us for a very long time but until we stop and listen to Him, we will not hear His distinctive call.

My name is Joseph George Hanna. I was born in Lebanon. My dad is Georges Hanna, my mother's name was Yvonne Sadaka. She died in the Lebanese War.

My parents came from a small town in the mountains called Tarshish. The town is close to the Bekaa Valley and to the city of Zahleh. We lived there in the summer but in the winter, because of the snow, we lived close to the sea and to the capital, Beirut, in a town called Byakoot.

My dad was a teacher, but before choosing that vocation, he wanted to be a priest. He went to the seminary at an early age but had bad problems with his eyes. This caused him to quit the seminary. He also worked for many years as a truck and bus driver. My mother was a housewife.

When my dad was in his twenties he married my mother who was only sixteen. They were not able to have children for five years. Since they lived in a small town where everyone knew everyone else, there was pressure on them to have children. It was a big struggle for them. My mother asked for the intercession of St. Abda Mechamar.

St. Abda was a disciple of St. Jude Thaddeus who

71

converted him while preaching in Persia. St. Jude ordained him a priest and then a bishop. Abda then went to Lebanon to preach the Gospel. At that time in Lebanon there were pagans who offered child sacrifices to their gods. Since the mothers were not allowed to cry for their babies, St. Abda would cry for the children. He once raised up a child from the dead and performed many other miracles. When a drought in the area was attributed to the saint's presence among them, they came to find out who the source of his power was. Which one of the gods did he believe in? For the pagans, it was known that Baal was the god of rain. When Abda preached Christ to them, thousands accepted the faith and asked to be baptized. However, there was no water for the Sacrament; but when Abda invoked the Baptism rite, it rained on them. Through his example and his miracles, St. Abda eventually became an intercessor for barren women and sick children. My mom went to the church devoted to St. Abda and spent all night there before the Blessed Sacrament. She saw in a dream that she would have a boy, then three girls, and then she would lose a boy. True to the dream, I was the first boy to come, followed by three younger sisters: Giselle, Antoinette, and Rula. We lost an unborn brother.

I gave him the name Antoine-Abda. It is good to know that I have a brother in heaven who is so close to me, loving me and praying for me always. I chose the name Antoine-Abda because my mother loved the name Anthony. She had a great devotion to St. Anthony of the Desert (AD 250) and St. Anthony of Padua (AD 1200). In gratitude to St. Anthony for his intercession, my mother dressed me in the habit of St. Anthony for an entire year. Already at the age of two, I had worn the Franciscan habit!

I did not like school in my childhood. It was not easy for me. We changed homes and schools many times because of the war. My dad told me when I was older that once I tried to avoid school by jumping out of the car. My parents tried another school, which my sisters and I liked better, even though I had to study many hours to do well.

In high school I did better, but it still took a lot of work for me to do well. At the university it took me some time to decide what I wanted to do. At first I wanted to go to Italy for architecture, but my parents were afraid I would marry an Italian girl and not return to Lebanon. I studied computer science in Lebanon instead. At the same time I opened a small deli business. This was a lot of work and I couldn't do my best in school because of the deli. The business was good but not the grades. I had a lot of anxiety because of school, business, and the war.

In Lebanon we had to go through many wars; I lost two cousins and other relatives. The war was scary with lots of bombing during the night. Many nights, we had to leave to go to a shelter when the enemy would start bombing our residential area at 2:00 or 3:00 a.m. Once, I was so scared that I hid behind a refrigerator because of the bombing and I begged God for a miracle. I remember this being my first prayer.

My mother was the foundation of faith in our family. She had an intimate relationship with the Lord. We could see this in her prayer and how she loved the poor. In spite of a back injury she would always help the poor. It was in my heart that one day I would serve the poor in Africa. She taught us how to pray the Rosary and different novenas. Sunday Mass was very important for my parents. I do not remember ever missing Mass. Sometimes we went to daily Mass too. But at that age I didn't pray well on my own, and I did not have a personal relationship with Jesus Christ. I was not sure about Confession, the Eucharist and the Mother of God, Mary. The good seed of my mother's example took a while to bear good fruit.

I was a person who was very attached to my friends, family, country, and especially to my mother. She was everything for me—she was like a god to me. She was a holy woman and gave me so much love and hope in my life.

Even with these strong attachments, I decided to run away from Lebanon—from the war, from the stress, from fear. I became a refugee in Canada. I thought that all my problems would end by being in a safe, stable place with many opportunities to work. When I was seven or eight years old, I loved the Canadian flag. I have no clue why—I did not even know that it was a flag. I had no idea that I would end up one day in that beautiful country. I believe the love of the flag and the desire to move to Canada was the work of God. He was preparing the way for my conversion. I am so grateful for all the help that I received from the government and the people of Canada.

But despite all this goodness, I was still seeking the wrong things in my life. My security was in my bank account and in feeling loved by my friends and my family. I had many wrong relationships.

In 1989, after I had been in Canada for about a year, my mother was injured by a bomb on August 15, the feast of Our Lady's Assumption. She died on August 22, the Queenship of Mary, after receiving Viaticum. Her death was unreal. I could not or did not want to believe it. Her death devastated me. I became hopeless and joyless, and cried many tears. I wanted just to die. I wanted to think that the death of my mother was a dream. I wanted to wake up from this nightmare and give my mother a call. It was so hard being a refugee and far away. I could not even attend her funeral.

During this time I worked as a computer programmer,

mainly for the government as a consultant. I tried to invest in a business that did not help me to have peace nor get close to Jesus. It was a night club. The name of that place was called Scandal, and it was a scandal for me. God still was not in the picture. I did not know Him as a person. I felt He was so distant from me. On Sundays I used to go church but my heart was not there. It was my choice to go to Mass even though I did not fully understand what was going on in the Sacrifice of the Mass. I felt bored in church but my hope was to meet a nice Lebanese girl who loved God. I believe I went to Mass, too, because of the example that my parents had given us.

By this time I was leading a life of sin. I felt stressed from work, from worrying about the future, from wrong relationships with women, from my attachment to my friends and from the loss of my mother. I felt empty most of the time. I was seeking the joy of the world, money, and impure sexual relationships. All of that did not fulfill me. It was like a flat tire that cannot be filled until it is fixed. The repair that I needed was meeting Jesus Christ as a person and falling in love with Him in the Eucharist, the Bread of Life. I had once heard a student in Lebanon saying that he was in love with Jesus, but I could not understand what he was talking about. How could anyone be in love with someone he cannot see?

I had many short relationships with women without committing to anyone. Every time I thought that I was in love it ended up with tragedy. After becoming intimate with someone I could not continue in the relationship. My physical attraction and my love for them did not last for long. I did not know that it was only emotion and not true love. Dating became like a nightmare for me. At that time I did not know that the Lord was preparing me for another path; to give my life to serve Him and His Church.

After working seven years in Canada, I met a team from the United States who suggested that I work in one of the southern states, where there was more money and better weather. I went to Florida, the Sunshine State, where I would eventually encounter the Light of Christ.

First I moved to West Palm Beach. After successfully completing a computer consulting contract, I returned to Lebanon. I tried different investments in Lebanon, hoping that I could stay close to my family. I invested in the construction of several apartments for sale or rent. I opened a computer shop, and worked on other investments. It was a bad time in Lebanon; the economy was not doing well.

At the same time my faith was still not there. My lack of faith was a source of more confusion for me. I did not know which direction I should take. I did not have a prayer life. I stopped going to Mass, claiming that I had no time. I thought I had to fix my problems before I could search for God. I remembered that I was given a statue of St. Joseph and an image of the Virgin Mother of God, Mary, for my office. I did not like the idea. I thought the statues would ruin the décor, and they had no value for me. I did not understand the purpose in having them. I tried to break the statue of St. Joseph and I hid the image of Mary.

Eventually, I went back to the United States to make more money. I went to Delray Beach, Florida, and I worked again as a computer programmer. Around this time I started to feel something in my heart. I became less upset about losing money in all my businesses.

One afternoon I was walking on the beach. The water touched my feet and I felt an unusual joy, like electricity, and I couldn't hide my joy. Every creature was telling me that God existed and that He was close to me. I was so happy. This inspiration repeated itself throughout the whole walk. I didn't understand it. I did not want people to see me laughing; they would think that I was crazy. Later, I understood that in Spanish, "Delray Beach" means "the beach of the king", where I had my first encounter with Christ the King.

Another experience I remember is that one day I was in my apartment in Tampa. While I was trying to listen to the news on an Arabic website, I heard the Maronite Mass instead. I was surprised to discover the beauty of the Mass. When the people were singing "Glory to God in the Highest and Peace to His people . . ., " I found it so beautiful. My heart was rejoicing. It was as if I had never listened to the Mass before. Was it God, or was it just that I missed my family and my language? I figured it was simply me missing home.

Another time, I asked myself a question: what would make me a happy person? If I have a million dollars on my desk, would it make me a happy person? Would the security of money change me? And the answer was no. I had another question. If God can create the most wonderful woman for me, does this make me a happy man? I was surprised that the answer was still no. I started to ask myself what I was looking for. If money and women could not make me happy, what would?

I began wanting to try living a chaste life. I was so surprised that I was able to do it day by day. I started to respect the dignity of women. I wanted to be pure in my relationships. I decided to wait for a sexual relationship until marriage. I thought it was by my own power that I could live this lifestyle. I did not realize that God's grace was at work in me to help me change. It started the day the Lord touched me in the water in Delray Beach—the beach of the king.

I had the desire to go back to church and to attend Mass at St. Paul, and later at Christ the King Parish in

Tampa. The Mass was very moving and beautiful. I felt that I was a different person, but this would not last.

I met a Christian girl who knew the Bible well; but sadly, I fell into sin again. She told me that St. Paul said in 1Cor. 6:9 that all those who live immoral lives will not see the kingdom of God.

I started to justify my sin by saying I was in love and there was nothing wrong with what I was doing. But I kept hearing the words that Jesus told Mary Magdalene, "Go and sin no more." God led me to a good, young adult retreat in Florida, which began a deeper change in me and gave me the grace to get away from every opportunity to sin. Now I understand that the Virgin Mary is the one who helped me the most with chastity and gave me respect for women. I am a child of her offspring as the Book of Revelation says in chapter twelve. The story of Our Lady of Fatima in Portugal led me to start praying the Rosary, contemplating the life of Christ and praying daily for the salvation of others. I started to go to daily Mass, frequent Confession, Bible study classes, and I watched religious videos. I developed a great devotion to the Holy Spirit and spent many hours praying before Jesus in the tabernacle. My desire to love and help my friends and neighbors grew.

But the Holy Spirit led me to the desert of temptation, just as Our Lord was tested after His Baptism. I went to Brazil for Christmas of 2000. It was a good test of my respect for women. After all the challenges, I seemed to pass the test, and my desire to be chaste continued. When I was flying back from the Rio de Janeiro airport, I started thinking about my next vacation, but another voice challenged my plan. I heard in my heart that I was very selfish. I was not concerned about other people. God showed me the poor in Brazil, but I was still concerned about my own entertainment. Did I really need to travel more? That question was very profound and vivid. It stayed with me. I made a promise to God by saying: Lord, I'm not going to travel any more for myself. I am going to travel only for You.

As time went by, I met someone special from my young adult prayer group. I was so attracted to her that I was thinking about marriage. I was happy to meet a good Christian girl who loved the Lord and wanted to live a holy life. But somehow, even with all the attraction to her, I could not see her as my wife and the mother of my children. We kept dating but we had no peace. We tried to take a break from the relationship.

In July 2001, a short time after that break, I was at work on a Saturday, trying to catch up with my responsibilities. By the way, Saturday is a special day for Our Lady and that particular date was close to the feasts of St. Mary Magdalene, St. Lawrence Brindisi, a Capuchin, St. Elijah the prophet, St. Charbel Makhlouf, and other saints that I loved. As I looked at the postcards of all the places that I had visited, the same voice I had heard in Rio came to me again: " You are so selfish; you think of yourself and not of Me." While wondering why God had given me so many opportunities to change my miserable life, I started writing down all these graces I had received: such as chastity, love of the Eucharist, trust in His mercy in Confession, love for the Bible and His words, Holy Hours where I would stay all night, great love for the Mother of God, Mary, who is full of grace, love of the life of the prophets and saints, and the desire to intercede for others.

All of a sudden I heard a voice in my heart: "What else could I do for you to know that I am calling you to Myself? If you do not say yes, point out to Me whom, according to you, should I call to sacrifice his life for Me?" I had tears of mixed feelings, to think that God was really calling me to Himself. I was a sinful man and I wanted to be married. I had never said yes until that moment. How could it be? At that moment I said yes without understanding how I could fulfill the words. What I remember is a great peace and many tears.

I confessed that Saturday to my prayer group that God was calling me to religious life. The next day I told my girlfriend about my call. It was very difficult for both of us.

I thought maybe God would make women ugly for me to be able to live this new life. I went to the mall and I saw a beautiful woman and I thought, You're killing me. I can't do this for all my life; it's too difficult.

After a while I tried to focus on my call but I was still testing the water, I guess. One day I was at a party and someone asked me to dance and I thought maybe I was not called after all. The next day I wanted to call that girl, but I did not have peace about it. I made a decision not to test my God and my vocation anymore. Our emotions are gifts from God, but we need to deal with them by reason and not by force. Some people do not understand our vocation. They ask us how we can abstain from sex. First, to abstain is a gift from God, and second, it is a directing of all our love to God who desires our spousal love. I learnt this later wiyh greater insight to help guide the natural desires of my heart and emotions.

I had never been interested in the priesthood. It seemed so lonely and sad. I had never met a holy priest in the past that I admired enough to be attracted to the vocation. I had heard of the Capuchin, Blessed Abouna Yaacoub, who came from an area close to my home town but I didn't know much about him. When I was a kid I had been attracted to the passion of Christ. I thought to if I saw the passion every day, my life would change. Also, as a boy, whenever I saw a religious habit, I liked that look. I also loved St. Francis of Assisi. I had true love and respect for him without knowing much about him.

In April 2002, I quit my job and did not want to return to work until I found my vocation. I could not ignore the call of serving God anymore, and was thinking about it day and night. I wanted to take all the time that I needed to understand what the next step in my life would be. After giving away some of my possessions in Tampa, Florida, I went to visit the community of the Franciscan Friars of the Renewal in NY.

After a great experience with the Friars in May, I left for Lebanon to discern religious life with the Maronite communities, the Capuchins and the Beatitudes with great hope that I would stay there. I was surprised that God did not give me the peace to enter into any of the communities in Lebanon. About my properties in Lebanon, the Lord led me to the Gospel of Luke, chapter 18. He told me that if I wantrd to follow Him, I needed to give my possessions to the poor. This reading of the Scripture was difficult and shocking to me. I did not have the courage to do it, and I found it very challenging for me in the beginning. I thought that I was not attached to my material things that I owned. But this calling of radical poverty showed me that I cannot let go easily of my security. At that moment I understood more about the story of the rich man who refused to give away his money, and why he went home sad. It was only by God's grace later in my life that I was at peace to let go. In the mean time I was constantly reminded of the experience that I had with the Friars in Harlem. In different churches that I visited I was reminded more than three times by the Lord when He sent the Disciples two by two "with nothing for the journey -- no staff, no bag, no bread, no money, no extra tunic." (Mark 6:7)

I could not ignore this radical calling and trusting in God's providence to preach His Gospel. Finally, I was encouraged by my spiritual director to return to NY for another visit. I managed to return in August for another two weeks. I was overwhelmed with joy when I arrived to St Joseph Friary. When my visit came close to an end I started to get sad in thinking of leaving, because I was told by the community that I needed to wait a year before entering postulancy (beginners). I was waiting with anguish to find out if the community would accept me to enter that year. Following a long series of discernment, psychological testing and interviews, the community accepted me in September of 2002. When that decision was made, I had an indescribable joy. It was the best gift that God could give me. I was the happiest man ever. I was and remain so joyful that God called me to serve Him—a call that I do not deserve. After dating so many women and never being able to commit to anyone, it was the first time I felt that I could commit to God with no hesitation. This spiritual joy continues to happen by God's grace with being a Franciscan Friar who serves God and the poor. There is nothing else I would rather do today than be a Friar who is in love with God and neighbor.

The formation period was like two rough stones rubbing against each other, one smoothing out the other. This experience will last for all my life as I live in community with others. The community is a great place to grow in love, to accept God's love, to give God all of my heart, and to love my neighbor as I love myself. Our daily schedule in community is:

6:00 a.m. First Prayer

6:30-7:30 a.m. Spiritual Reading

7:30-8:30 a.m. Morning Prayer and the Sacrifice of the Mass

The Eucharist gives food for the soul, followed by a time of thanksgiving for the Bread of Life.

Breakfast (food for the body) follows Mass.

Each brother has different duties during the day. My responsibility was to beg for the needs of the Friary. This was also time to meet new friends in the marketplace and preach the good news of Jesus Christ.

12:00 p.m. Midday Prayer followed by lunch, after which we go out again.

5:00-6:00 p.m. Evening Prayer with a Holy Hour (Exposition of the Blessed Sacrament) followed by an hour for supper.

9:15 p.m. Night Prayer with Rosary followed by respectful silence until breakfast the next day.

We avoid conversation and try to hear Our Lord speaking to us in silence.

After six years with the community I made my final vows of poverty (only Jesus is what I need), chastity (only Jesus is my love), and obedience (only Jesus is my boss). After a long discernment I was accepted to the seminary to study further for the priesthood. I love the Mass deeply, and I desire to bring God's mercy to others in Confession. So even though I never liked studying, I now find it a sweet cross. It's not easy to go to the dentist, but in the end you will have a healthy mouth. It takes me a long time to grasp difficult concepts. It is joyful despite all the challenges. I remember once complaining about learning Greek when I didn't do well. The Lord said, "Silence. Open a Bible in Greek now. Tell Me if you can understand." I said, "I can." He replied, "I am spending so much money on you and I am giving you good information." After that I just said, "I will do my best, Lord, and please do Your part. If I don't do well that's okay for my humility."

I like to intercede by name for the other seminarians, and for the staff and faculty, and especially for my brothers in the community. I have a few more years, but I am excited to learn not only philosophy and theology, but also psychology so I can better help God's people. I want to participate in God's mercy and fulfill what Jesus says, *"I was hungry and you gave me to eat. . . ."* (Mt: 25:35)

Marriage is a beautiful and holy vocation but the Lord asked me to give my life for Him. I cherish my calling very much. I couldn't be happy or at peace unless I did God's will with love and passion. I would not be happier if I were married because God had always a better plan for me.

I end with the quotation from the Song of Solomon that shows the amazing love of God for us. Jesus' love for us in the Bread of Life, the Eucharist, is shown beautifully in these lines from the Song of Songs:

Let him kiss me with the kisses of his mouth,
for your love is more delightful than wine.

You are all-beautiful, my beloved,
and there is no blemish in you.
Come from Lebanon, my bride,
come from Lebanon, come!
You have ravished my heart, my sister, my bride;
you have ravished my heart
with one glance of your eyes,
with one bead of your necklace.
How beautiful is your love, my sister, my bride,
how much more delightful is your love than wine,
and the fragrance of your ointments than all spices!
Set me as a seal on your heart,
as a seal on your arm;
For stern as death is love,
relentless as the nether world is devotion;
its flames are a blazing fire.
Deep waters cannot quench love,
nor floods sweep it away.
Were one to offer all he owns to purchase love,
he would be roundly mocked.

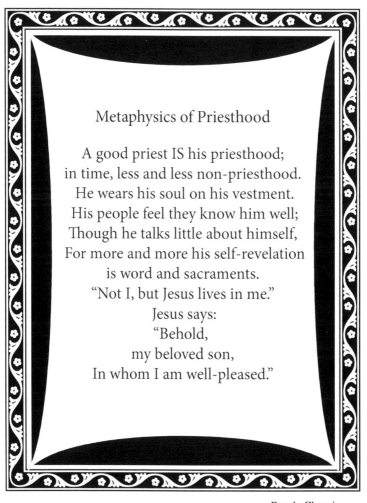

Metaphysics of Priesthood

A good priest IS his priesthood;
in time, less and less non-priesthood.
He wears his soul on his vestment.
His people feel they know him well;
Though he talks little about himself,
For more and more his self-revelation
is word and sacraments.
"Not I, but Jesus lives in me."
Jesus says:
"Behold,
my beloved son,
In whom I am well-pleased."

Ronda Chervin

87

88

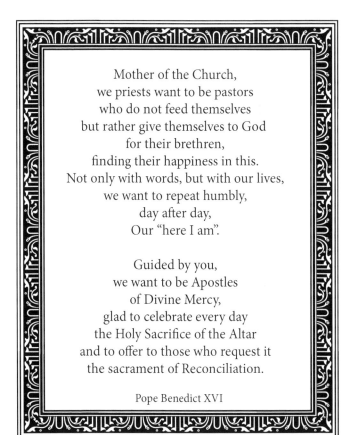

Mother of the Church,
we priests want to be pastors
who do not feed themselves
but rather give themselves to God
for their brethren,
finding their happiness in this.
Not only with words, but with our lives,
we want to repeat humbly,
day after day,
Our "here I am".

Guided by you,
we want to be Apostles
of Divine Mercy,
glad to celebrate every day
the Holy Sacrifice of the Altar
and to offer to those who request it
the sacrament of Reconciliation.

Pope Benedict XVI

Only God Works Like This!

Bob Schikora

*The many detours of a life may seem to be roadblocks.
But as Bob Schikora relates, even lengthy detours will
lead us to our original destination if we let them.*

I was born in Detroit, Michigan in 1947 to a family of German ancestry that was idyllically, fervently Catholic. My younger sister and I enjoyed growing up in our middle class, Catholic neighborhood where our whole lives centered around the parish and school. The kids I played with were mostly Catholic and most of us attended Catholic high schools as well.

At Immaculate Heart of Mary Grade School, we all attended Mass every day. The boys would begin serving Mass in fifth grade. I loved it. I felt drawn to the priesthood then but there were a couple of reasons I didn't go to the minor seminary (high school seminary) after eighth grade.

For one thing, at that time, I was a severe stutterer. My parents generously got me speech therapy but I really didn't use the techniques I learned there until years later. Though I wasn't refused entrance to the minor seminary because of my stammer, going would have been a high mountain to climb.

Another reason for not entering minor seminary was that I really loved instrumental music. I had taken clarinet lessons in grade school but my real love was percussion. Catholic Central High School had a great band and I really wanted to go there. It was marching band in the fall for football season and symphonic band in winter and spring. Life was good. I had a girlfriend, I had band, and I loved Catholic Central.

My high school was run by the Basilian Fathers. At that time, the Basilians were mainly high school and college teachers. They were really dedicated priests and very involved with the students. Classes ended at 3:00 p.m., but the activities went on every day well into the night. By the time my senior year came around, I was thinking about joining their community. I experienced a great peace about this decision. My stuttering was somewhat improved though still severe. I was encouraged to enter the novitiate and keep working on it.

I began training with the Basilian Fathers in August 1965 after graduation. The formation period takes many years and so there was plenty of time for speech improvement and discernment. Life that first year was very strict. It was monastic in many ways. There were no TVs, no phones, no radios, no newspapers, and only four family visiting days in the entire year! The novitiate is designed to be a transitional year from secular life to religious life. Despite its challenges, I would not trade it for anything. It anchored me in my faith for life. It also blessed me with life-long friends. We had Mass, prayer, Liturgy of the Hours, formation classes, work and recreation. The day ended with more prayer and Grand Silence. You never had to worry about what you would do. It was all laid out for you. After I got used to the routine, I began to like it.

By the end of the year, we were a band of brothers. Even now, the brothers from those years are among my closest friends. Seventy out of eighty took temporary vows of poverty, chastity, and obedience. The next year we were moved on to houses of study at various Catholic colleges.

In my freshman year as a scholastic at college, I started to realize I didn't really want to be a teacher. Music was still tugging at me and I didn't have any specific route to teach music as a religious. At the end of the year, I told my superior that, even though it had been a great time for me, I didn't want to continue. I decided to go back home to Detroit and continue school there.

The only university I could afford was Wayne State in downtown Detroit. I remember my dad, a building tradesman, saying: "Bob, I can't afford to help you with tuition but I can get you a job in the trade as an apprentice pipe insulator. That will help you pay your bills." By the time I graduated from college, I was also a journeyman pipe insulator.

Once home, I also started to date. The old girlfriend was gone, but there were other girls I knew from high school. I started dating one of them exclusively while working and going to school. We dated for three years, got engaged, and were married in 1970.

I think, because my spiritual life had been well-formed as a Basilian, when I married, I remained very grounded in the Faith. We always went to Sunday Mass and our extended families were still actively practicing Catholics. We had two children and my wife eventually got a Ph.D. in modern languages. There were no good teaching jobs near Detroit so she decided to go on to law school. She was a brilliant student. Her career after law school was very successful.

By now the kids were in high school, and my wife was a full partner in a law firm. In contrast, I did not like school. After college, where I had majored in business, I entered the coast guard as a junior officer. In addition to music, the water was my other great interest.

I was actually assigned to active duty in Detroit. It was perfect: Our families were there and I knew the waters and vessels of the area. Through the coast guard, I really got to know the Port of Detroit. After my active duty was completed, I eventually became a tugboat captain there. I really enjoyed the work but the hours and time away from home were bad for a father of two children.

When the Detroit Fire Department built a new fireboat, I was hired as one of the captains. The schedule was great: one day on, two off, one on, two off, one on, and five off. This left me with lots of time to be with the kids and have a great job too. But after four years I was laid off for lack of city funding. It was during this time that I also earned my unlimited tonnage, U.S. Coast Guard First Class Pilot's License. Fortunately, when the fire department layoff occurred, I was able to get a job piloting large, deep-sea ships in the Detroit River and Lake Erie area. That job lasted for three and a half years.

Just before becoming a permanent pilot, I had a two minor incidents. Neither was serious. However, any incident before becoming a permanent pilot was career-threatening. I decided to leave the pilot association rather than risk being asked to leave.

This change was quite devastating. I had worked for years to prepare for this career and now it was gone. With piloting over, instead of making good money with a prestigious job to match my wife's spectacular career, I was back to insulating pipe—full circle to my first job!

In retrospect I see that, had I stayed with the ships, I would probably not be preparing for the priesthood now. In an attempt to recover, I applied and was accepted at the University of Michigan for post-graduate work in percussion. Perhaps I could still teach that. It was a most challenging time, but also one with great memories. I got into the Michigan Marching Band and had a wonderful experience. By this time I was forty-two and my wife and her friends thought I was in a mid-life crisis and doing something juvenile. I loved it. But after a successful academic year, my dean warned me of poor job prospects at my age.

I left school and decided to open my own business. I bought a dilapidated store on the Michigan campus near the football stadium and made it into a deli: Michigan Bandstand Deli. I owned and operated it for three years. I had great customers and employees, but I worked night and day and made nothing. My wife supported the family from her law practice.

Now, in the mid-nineties, my kids and wife stopped practicing their Catholic Faith. We were suffering as a family, and I didn't clearly see all of the reasons why. I was praying more than ever.

After finally selling the deli business and building, I opened a kayak business. I was back to the water again and that went better than the deli but still did not generate enough income to support the family. I went back to the pipe insulation trade again. That was when my wife got tired of my lack of success, and, after thirty years of marriage, said she wanted a divorce! I pleaded with her to no avail.

I moved to my own place, and after a year decided to start the annulment process. I remember thinking that if I did meet someone else, being married in the Church was most important. It took almost two years for the archdiocese to get to our file. We received a Decree of Nullity because of factors in our dating and engagement time which were judged to be real impediments to a sacramental marriage.

I know many people think that such annulments are decreed by Church tribunals just out of laxity. This is simply not the case. I am convinced that this tribunal was very thorough and that the procedure was valid. The work of a tribunal is an instrument of God's mercy and healing.

Now I was in my mid-fifties. I met a very attractive woman at a course in ballroom dancing that I was taking just for fun. She turned out to be a fervent Catholic who attended daily Mass. Her devotion to the Eucharist and to Mary was very inspiring. Through our relationship, I also started going to daily

Mass. She encouraged me to begin taking courses in philosophy and theology at Sacred Heart Seminary to deepen my understanding of the Faith even more. It worked.

Eventually, after four years, our relationship ended. She had been God's instrument in preparing me for what was coming. I was still searching for answers. In prayer, I asked Jesus, I know that You want me to do something in the Church. Show me what.

I thought maybe I would be suited to the permanent diaconate, but I was not at all sure. In January 2007, I went the March for Life in Washington, D.C. There, to my surprise, I met a priest from the Basilian house of studies where I had been assigned as a young man. It was Fr. Douglas Mosey, CSB. I asked him what he was doing these days and he told me he was the rector of a seminary in Cromwell, Connecticut. I told him I was still searching.

Then in March, in one of my classes at Sacred Heart, I met a man with gray hair who was a late-vocation seminarian for the Diocese of Saginaw. We became friends. His name is Bill Spencer (now Father Bill Spencer). He was a widower. One day he said to me, "Bob, I want to get this straight. You're single and you think you are called to some sort of service in the Church. . . .Why don't you be a priest?"

" I thought I was too old!"

He replied, "Would you talk to my bishop?"

"Well," I said, "if a bishop will talk to me, of course I would talk to your bishop."

Three nights later Bishop Robert Carlson (now Archbishop of St. Louis) was opening a huge charismatic conference in Detroit. I decided to stand in back and see who he was. He opened the conference with a prayer and then started moving toward the back of the large hall. My friend spotted me. He waved me over to meet Bishop Carlson. He introduced me to the bishop as someone discerning a vocation.

The bishop looked right into my eyes and took my hand in a firm shake and said, "I will pray for you."

The next morning my friend called and said, "Bishop Carlson wants to talk to you. Bring a one page, single-spaced vita of your life, good and bad."

Two days later I met the bishop again. He talked to me for two and a half hours. I told him everything.

At the end he said, "Bob, here's what I want you to do. Lent is coming up. Stay as close to the sacraments as possible with your work. When Easter is over I want you to come and see me again. If some day you can even offer one Mass and hear one Confession, it would all be worth it."

During the drive home I was almost shaking. He had left the door open for the priesthood. I did as he asked. After some weeks I was moved to make an application. I didn't know this at the time, but I was told later that this bishop has the practice of putting files received from seminary applicants on the altar during his prayer time for seven days. He asks the Holy Spirit, "Do you want this guy or not?"

I came back after Easter and he asked me, "How are you doing with all of this?"

I answered, "I feel this peace."

He said, "So do I. Welcome to the Diocese of

Saginaw!"

I left that meeting almost shaking. I was overwhelmed that my past didn't make it impossible to become a priest. In the course of my talks with Bishop Carlson, somehow it came out that I had met Fr. Mosey. Bishop Carlson knows Fr. Mosey well.

He picked up the phone and called Fr. Mosey in Connecticut and said, "I'm sending Bob Schikora to you." So, by the fall of 2007, I was happily beginning seminary studies. Recently I was ordained a transitional deacon for the Diocese of Saginaw by Bishop Joseph Cistone, our new Ordinary.

God willing, I will be ordained a priest in May, 2011. Throughout my journey I have experienced great support and prayers from my adult children, family, friends, and brother seminarians. I have experienced more joy in the Lord than I could ever have dreamed.

(Note from Dr. Ronda Chervin: Fr. Schikora was ordained May 20, 2011 for the Diocese of Saginaw.)

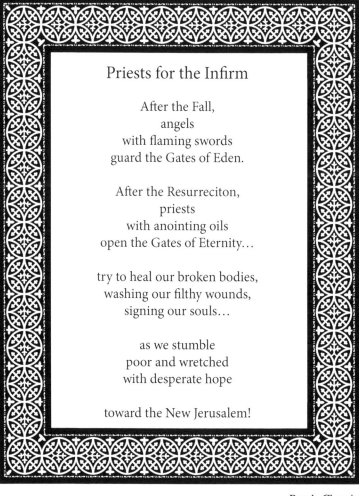

Priests for the Infirm

After the Fall,
angels
with flaming swords
guard the Gates of Eden.

After the Resurreciton,
priests
with anointing oils
open the Gates of Eternity…

try to heal our broken bodies,
washing our filthy wounds,
signing our souls…

as we stumble
poor and wretched
with desperate hope

toward the New Jerusalem!

Ronda Chervin

Advocate and Mediatrix of grace,
you who are fully immersed
in the one universal mediation of Christ,
invoke upon us, from God,
a heart completely renewed
that loves God with all its strength
and serves mankind as you did.
Repeat to the Lord
your efficacious word:
"They have no wine",
so that the Father and the Son
will send upon us
a new outpouring of
the Holy Spirit.
Full of wonder and gratitude
at your continuing presence in our midst,
in the name of all priests
I too want to cry out:
"Why is this granted me,
that the mother of my Lord
should come to me?"

Pope Benedict XVI

Gin Game Interrupted

Lars Markham

Great gifts, even great energy are a great responsibility. Lars shows us though, how even these talents are not enough. Only when he listens closely to God and how He might want those gifts to be used, (and perhaps not in the most glamorous fashion), does Lars begin to focus on what might ultimately be most satisfying.

"Where you're born is an accident. But it's your responsibility to find the place where you belong."
—Helmut Jahn, Architect

Sometime in my late 30's, I found the above quote in a Southern California business publication, and it *struck me* in the most powerful, *eye opening manner possible… and concurrently*, I felt that I had *really gotten it!*

Today in my mid 50's, I now know the nomenclature of the experience to be a solid, true version of a **valid moment**. This is defined as a moment, *quite distinctive from all other moments,* due to its momentous significance and incredible stature. *Time seems to stand still here.* Feelings of *wonderfulness* can exist.... Something small, *but special, fits* the bill also... *richness of experience* that stops the flow of temporality surfaces as really *the very depth of being itself,* as opposed to non-being.

I have now come to learn so many things in my mid 50's. *The meaning* of a *valid moment,* as delineated above, was extracted from a lecture given by Dr. Ronda Chervin . *The meaning* to me *today* of the opening quote, does however, inherently contain *one word* that *today*, I find I would like to tangentially *recast* to reflect my progressively spiritually enhanced way of comprehending the world at this life juncture. While I cannot today say that where we are born *is an accident*, as I feel that we are born into our *specific sitz-in-leben, life setting*, for very *specific reasons...* I do feel that it is our responsibility to find the place where we *will later* belong... *but, however*, with God's grace in helping us *live out His will for us.*

My life story is very, very much about acknowledgment of these true, *valid moments* that have transpired, as these *moments* accurately reflect incredible junctures and transitions in my life plan that have led to wondrous tangents, adventures, extrapolations of general themes, and distinct component voyages that have made me *who I am* today.

You see, I now understand, *and accept,* that I *do not know* how the story ends, and my imagination may in fact have come up with intermediate and final scenes, that in essence, *are truly underwhelming*…. I now know, it is far, far better, to leave the big picture parts to God and His will, and to listen carefully for potential script progressions, and to be ready to follow along vibrantly as you master your present lines and become ready for the next scene… Your conscience/window to the Spirit, *is your avenue* to the *right script*, and the respective component parts in life….

Maybe now this is the right time *to let you in on* some of the *past sagas, endeavors, and developments* that have occurred so far in my *journey* through life, and I'll also *attempt* to *forecast* a bit on where God may be taking me at this crucial *valid moment* I now find myself within as I write these life progression passages.

Let's go back in time a bit to the mid 1950's when I entered this world. I was born into a family of a German immigrant father and a New York-born mom who was the daughter of Sicilian immigrants. My youngest years were spent in the Little Italy quadrant of lower Manhattan where my mother's two sisters and brother, along with their respective families, all lived together in various apartments in a brownstone that my mother's parents had bought after settling in New York. I do not remember much of this period; in addition to my young age, I also needed strong glasses by the time I was four.

A subsequent move to the central Bronx then occurred followed by a move to the far northeast Bronx at the Long Island Sound in first grade. Now I've finally reached the point where I can start remembering family things that might be more significant for this late-vocation treatise. The years in the northeast Bronx, at this *then-seaside cottage atmosphere*, are now remembered, *in a Monday morning quarterback kind of way*, as the place where I first discovered *beauty in the world*. This is a key revelation, as it will set the stage for so many of my aspirations, goals, and visions sought throughout my life.

My parents, later in life, both became increasingly good painters, and it was so clear that they both had harbored inborn talents earlier in life. *In flashbacks*, I recognize that I knew about their talents at this time in the years of my early formation. My father's greatest pleasure was in working on various private contract jobs in painting, woodworking, gold leafing and

renovation. My mother was a great gardener/
landscaper, and actually quite talented in interiors,
including the proportion and juxtaposition of
objects. I have one older sister, and she also
witnessed and absorbed much design talent from
our surroundings, which she utilized well in both
the fashion and the exterior and interior home
design arenas. I witnessed incredible attention to
detail that my father displayed in his work, as well
as a great sense of color matching and application
technique.

Our modest cottage home was filled with rather
creative objects that appeared even more unique
through great placement and spatial balance. My
mother impeccably tended to the front terraced
gardens, and unique, delicately flowering
vegetation even flourished well in the crevices of
the stone retaining walls that secured the various
terracing levels. Views of the Long Island Sound
beyond were framed well by arbors and trellises
enveloped by clinging masses of rose and grape
vine. The bucolic setting was a perfect splice of
Nantucket and the Amalfi, interwoven into one
highly imaginative, conjectural illusion... *And also
here*, I learned more of what made beauty when

being granted a beagle puppy we named Bullet, who was always happy and there for me with *unconditional love*. Such was the *sitz-in-leben* if you will, where the *beauty in the world* first really became apparent to me, and what I would later come to understand to be the *cataphatic* way of knowing of God and of His existence.

In sixth grade, my parents, Bullet, and I moved into Manhattan, and here my life would change quite dramatically. My sister had left home at the time we moved to the cottage by the Sound, and already had been living in Manhattan where she was a furrier executive. Her career had started in modeling, but she became more interested in the business and management aspects of the industry, and would later head up that company as well as progressively larger women's sportswear corporations in future years.

My sister always played *by her own rules*, and *was and is* kind of a mix of the Haley Mills character in *The Trouble with Angels*, Woody Allen's *Annie Hall*, *Auntie Mame* and Margaret Thatcher all rolled into one. It really depended on the time of day, mood, work, and relationship involvement at the time. Being eleven years my elder, she was my version of Auntie Mame in my elementary school years. She exposed me to a dazzling world of both *beauty* and *glamour*, which at times were *one and the same*, and at times, *quite, quite* different. *Quite easy* to comprehend today, but *quite difficult* to discern then. I also remember her remarking that *life was like a country club*, where one should partake in *only the activities* that one found of interest. She has lived/lives by this motto *quite, quite* successfully.

During this time period of my life (that I will delineate as being from sixth grade through to twelfth grade), my exposure to the *supposed best of life,* thrust forward full blast. Through my sister, and by way of Mom and Dad through the venue of living on the upper east side of Manhattan, I became familiar and quite comfortable with the better elements of American materialism. I fortunately was able to discriminate, though, what *I did actually like*, as opposed to what *I was told to like* by American society. My tastes leaned in the direction of the strata of rather understated composition and element, as opposed to ostentatious exemplifications of such, *aimed at times by some* to impress others in arena spectacles of conspicuous consumption. *I knew what I liked, and why……* and it ranged from rather ordinary but unique items, to quite sophisticated and highly coveted items.   Travel on the international front only heightened my exposure and evolving, discriminating taste level when journeying to Europe, the Caribbean and Latin America during those years.   I also decided I wished to major in architecture when entering college, and this would take me to even more higher levels of exposure to both the *more refined* as well as *the more crude* rudiments and trappings in life.

Concurrently, *thank God*, I did have the ultimate grounding wire in life, as I had incredibly strong faith and solid belief in God. My mother was a practicing Catholic, and my father a German Lutheran who converted to Catholicism when marrying my mother. Church on Sundays was very much a part of our lives, although I do remember many times around fifth and sixth grade walking a considerable distance to Church alone. I always found comfort there, and for the most part, made it there most Sundays. I also found solitude, reflection, peace and God's presence during long, long walks in attractive urban and rural areas, and have continued to seek out this escape/outlet all throughout my later years to present day.

Career definition, planning, and execution, also commenced unassumingly during this period, and would come to be one of the most passionate, frustrating, joyous, perplexing, imaginative, depressing, exciting, underwhelming and explosive arenas in life on which I chose to focus *exceedingly*. Little did I know in these earlier years, that I would evolve into the *component builder* type of guy, where nothing by itself *was really ever enough*, and that I would constantly need to reach the *next plateau* and *tangential branching* in order to yield *some type of satisfaction* in my endeavors and perceived progressions. Money would not be the motivator, **fortunately**/*unfortunately*, depending on the week one asked that question. *Perhaps*, five percent of the time, it *might have* been. But five percent will never allow one to *pull the game off* successfully, and do *whatever* it takes**, fortunately**...

Somehow then, I decided to focus on the architectural profession, which has been a great source of happiness, obsession, creativity, depression, euphoria and stagnation at times over the periods of actual practice *and beyond...* Architecture would appear then to combine *the beauty aspects* I now see that were quite prevalent in my upbringing, and the creativity I seemed to harbor that needed to be channeled appropriately. I did, however, research the field enough to know that it was unstable, for the most part low paying, sporadic in work flow and most of the time, mundane and mechanical.

I still decided to pursue training in such, and from one of *the top* high schools in New York, I then went on to one of *the top* Catholic institutions of higher learning in the United States to pursue a degree in architecture. Strong interests in high school existed also in the math areas, and this would later become a source of conflict, as my career desires needed to span both areas in a significant manner in order for me to achieve some sense of self-fulfillment and progression.

I do b*elieve I was listening for God's plan* at this point, as the feelings *did come from way inside*, and I *clearly sought out* a Catholic institution of higher learning for my undergraduate studies. After being at a secular high school that *in my opinion*, did *not stress* the *love of learning*, but *unconsciously perha*ps did stress the love of materially moving up in the world, I unequivocally sought to strengthen my Catholic identity further. Guidance counseling at the highly acclaimed secular high school was basically worthless, and I even sensed a bit of anti-Christian undertone when it was clear where I would be attending undergraduate studies. *Not my problem at all* though, as *I knew where I belonged,* and I sense the Holy Spirit was guiding me at this point as the warm feelings for attending were coming from way inside of me.

I did unfortunately, however, at this point, begin to acquire what I now label as the *American media gut,* which followed American popular culture and constantly tried to force upon me things that *I did not want,* but was told *that I should want and aspire to*... I mean if one *did not* want *more and more,* then something was clearly wrong with one's motivation, industriousness, ambition and drive, and these were clear signs of an underachiever... *A bit misguided* in translation actually, and I did sense this transgression forging its way inside of me, but fortunately I was strong enough to combat it... *at least then,* and *for the most part*, all throughout my life…

The years spent studying architecture were nothing less than fanta*bulous*…   Great *mind expansion* exercises, a year in Europe, classmates and faculty who were some of the brightest around, great real learning atmosphere inherently demonstrating the *love of learning* I had been seeking, etc. etc. etc… My studies and love of design and architectural history dominated my life both at home and abroad. I would not consider myself *then or now* as arrogant, but I did sense and was reminded repeatedly through comments of others, that I had some great gifts bestowed on me by God. I was considered   bright,   astute,   tall,   personable, attractive, witty, deep, artistic, caring, and creative.

I kept the knowledge to myself, and do not feel *for the most part*, that I ever used these qualities in a most discordant manner at all. I will admit though, that when feeling insecure at times for *whatever reason*, I did go *out on the market* so to speak, to see where I stood and ranked. *Knowing* I could attain something or *whatever*, would always be enough for me, and I never really had to   go through the motions to attain something I did not really want, or need, simply to prove to *myself or others* that *I could get it.*

I did, though, tenaciously go after what it was *that I did want*, but only after reflection, to affirm to myself that it was *good,* and not at all of even a spark of somewhat malicious intention. *I had/have a conscience and a soul*, and would always be guided by such, whether I wanted *this to be or not...* it was simply *who I was... And*, I would never knowingly, take advantage of others, for business, pleasure or *whatever...*

I wanted my business dealings to be win/wins, if at all possible, otherwise I would want *wins*, but in an orthodox manner...Woman friends and acquaintances were labeled off limits to me, *by me*, unless I would seriously be considering *one* as potential marriage material, and *then* I wanted to learn more, and therefore would develop a stronger relationship, etc...   Possessions were definitely desired, but only items I found of incredible interest, and had thought over incessantly at times, almost *ad nauseum.*

I do admit later on in life, at times wanting and *securing* things that were generally perceived *as hard to get*, but again only if I truly wanted them after *much intense internal examination.* The practice of my faith was not handled surreptitiously at all, and was quite open.... And I had placed myself in the perfect atmosphere to do so, again with the grace, I believe, of the Holy Spirit.

My life would then continue to be defined by periods of *educational enhancement* dividing long periods of *professional development.* Effortlessly, turbulently, peacefully, dynamically, and haphazardly, all moved along rapidly, meanderingly, sporadically and articulately.

On the love circuit, I never met the *right woman*, in *my opinion*, and *never approached* the situation as some business deal that would have a deadline. I simply felt that if it were meant to be, it would *simply happen*. Perhaps naïve, but again *how* I had felt/feel. What I *absolutely knew I did not want*, was to engage in a marriage with the *wrong woman*. I had/have seen this consistently throughout my life *all around me*, and I had more than ample opportunities to play this aspect of the *Gin Game*, if you will. Starter marriages, sophisticated affairs, complicated interludes and open marriages, were just not in my vocabulary, and I would never want to enter a marriage thinking that it would not be *till death do us part.* Just not my M.O.

I do admit *that I myself* complicated the search immensely by *overtly* admitting quite honestly *to myself and others, that I* did not want children at *any point soon* and potentially, *never; that I* was very into my career development and wanted *to do whatever felt right, whenever;* and *that I* wanted to live in a *perceived dignified manner, exactly where I wanted;* that I wanted to travel extensively to fabulous, intoxicatingly beautiful and inspirational places especially of flawless natural beauty that at times might be classified as *sybaritic* by some; *and that basically* I had *an agenda* and wanted to *explore it, live it, and develop it* to the *higher levels....*

The problem exists here in that basically *I was/am a good, honest guy,* but as I say, I *had an agenda,* and really wanted to *go with it* and see *where it led...* baby diapers really were not part of it, and neither was a life in some mid-American suburb, in some mundane, non-passionate job/mid-management position, with *possible* vacation trips to an American Redneck Riviera...I wanted *so, so much more,* and wanted *to travel* the before mentioned route *as the way* to some sense of fulfillment and peace....

Another goal, would be *to find the perfect place* to retire to later in life, although the word retirement was also never in my vocabulary. I really wanted to find and develop the perfect gig that I could continue on with, *someday, in the perfect place, and ride with into the sunset .... Anyway,* on such a *quest*, one does come in contact with *many, many women* that *seek the same*, but many may/ have been variations of *como se dice,* gold diggers, meal ticket seekers, etc. etc. No interest for me of those in *questa categoria*. Not that there aren't some really great women with these same desires as I had, *as there clearly are*, and at times, I have met them...but various factors like living 6000 miles away, her being married already, my not being *Mr. Right*, not having my head on straight that week, wrong place/wrong time, etc. foreclosed on continuing dialogue, etc.

I am blessed though to have always had great women friends in my life, and some that I have known for forty years or more.... They are *true friends*, and we have never had any, again, *como se dice, complications,* that would compromise the relationship, thus creating the situation where it could not develop to the ultimate *best friends* level that I have attained with some of *the guys*. Anyway, ...

So life *meanderingly* and *ploddingly,* moved on through some wild cycles and whirlwinds, plots and *secretive* sub-plots, triumphs and fiascos, progressions and setbacks, etc. etc. etc. After completing my bachelor of architecture, I relocated to Ft. Lauderdale where my parents were residing. I *quickly secured* a position in a *premier* architectural firm in the area, and *quickly decided* that re-designing the skins of select barrack type, leisure villa complexes, from Dutch Colonial to Spanish Mediterranean to Moorish Moroccan, *was not really* what I had pictured as a great architectural platform from which to develop my embryonic career. I also *quickly decided*, that Ft. Lauderdale was not the answer to my problem, and even though I saw myself cast into a vivacious, truly fulfilling lifestyle in the tropics, this was clearly not the postcard I wished to *time warp* into full speed.... Instead, I pulled the throttle, and jet propelled myself right out of there, and to the semi, semi, *well not really, paradise* of Chicago....

Chicago, *in the mid/late 70's, was a great town for an architect*, and I had lots of friends there from undergrad life. I took my portfolio on the road, and did the *Go See* game of cruising from office to office to see if they needed to add staff. One firm, which turned out to be a well-respected engineering house that also did architectural work, did need help and wanted to move more into the design arenas. They liked what I *brought to the table*, and I joined after what turned out to be a relatively quick search.

I rented a great glass walled/windowed apartment overlooking one of the harbors along Lake Shore Drive, (again *beauty was key* to me, and a *must have*), and the *career* transpired onward. Great firm, great people, and solid, good breaks and opportunities in office, residential and the hospitality design sectors. *My parents however were slightly* concerned *one day* when I told them that during the first week of work *one morning*, the *trip on LSD took one hour*. I then *retracted* the statement when I realized that *shock had set into my mom*, and then quickly p*araphrased* the statement to say *that the bus ride down Lake Shore Drive to the Loop, took one hour that morning.*

I *grew up fast* in Chicago, and loved it there, securing a solid professional life as well as a great support group of friends. A few years later though, a major recession hit town causing the firm to run out of work, and out the door a good number of us eventually went to seek employment where our backgrounds might be needed. I had very strong faith at this point, and got through this ordeal relatively quickly due to my flexibility for a career switch.

As mentioned I had always enjoyed math and subsequently the investment areas, and I was able to secure a position at a major national retail brokerage house as a financial advisor trainee. (*I think they were simply called stockbrokers in those days*). I became licensed after passing all the exams, and started canvassing the markets for clients. All began to fall in place well, as I was found to have strong marketing talents and wore well with people. One problem surfaced though in that I *really did not want to sell what I ultimately did not believe in. This would continue to surface all throughout life* for me. *In that environment*, it was very, very hard to find someone who cared about *a perceived small obstacle such as that*, and

I then left to take on a new challenge in Houston, in architectural design and real estate syndication.

Houston was *not Chicago* in so, so many ways....The movie Urban Cowboy, was *in my opinion*, not a movie but a *documentary*. A brief *test drive* in highway living, parking garage designs at work, ribs, and other venues I can't really describe properly without being totally disrespectful, and off I was again. Helping me to see the light more clearly, was the event of seeing *yet another* giant, *como se dice*, 'wood roach' the morning of my twenty-seventh birthday.

I spontaneously decided that this was *no place to spend my twenty-seventh birthday*, and had the movers come that afternoon after giving notice at work that morning, and also informing the landlord that I would never adjust to the local *fauna* of the area, and really preferred to *live alone* at this point. *I took the red eye that night, to the next destination....*

New York, where my sister and her husband graciously gave me shelter literally, *at a mere moment's notice. Miraculously*, I found architectural work within just a few short days in a well-regarded national firm, and *miraculously* again, secured an apartment in my parents building in the Turtle Bay area of midtown right off United Nations Plaza. (Florida also turned out *not to be* the answer for my parents' problem either, and my mother especially missed the pedestrian orientation of Manhattan and the ease of attainment of services, diversions, etc.)

Some good, varied experience was attained at that architecture shop, when yet another *recessional* layoff surfaced again, and *this guy* decided *that he had* simply, **had it**....I decided that I was *out of this field*, and planned on attaining an MBA and establishing a more stable life, with progressive opportunities at *hopefully one organization*, where I might be able to move *up the ladder* and have my job evolve into a senior, upper management position one day.

A natural progression to architecture is the tangential real estate business area of finance, development and investment management, and fortunately I was accepted at *arguably the top* real estate MBA program in the country. *Miraculously again*, a position surfaced in national corporate real estate development work for a top tier, global financial services firm, and I was selected for this job due to my combined architectural and brokerage background. *Great interim gig* until B School began.

The Graduate real estate program I chose was small, quite selective, and *accepting for the most part, returning students with advanced degrees* in law, architecture. engineering as well as the other business areas. Great program, great profs and *great, great real estate head*. We hit it off immediately, and I evolved into one of the best *highest and best use analysis, feasibility/ appraisal* people in the program. My thesis was selected as the top entry, and given to the local community for a re-development project in which they were seeking our evaluative assistance.

When pondering where I would land after graduation, I thought I might want to enter the investment banking/syndication arena. The real estate head *laughed*, said he really did not see me as a wh--e, and said he'd get me an interview at a *top, top* Wall Street shop, *under one condition*....that I tell him afterward why I *would not want the job*.... I reluctantly agreed, and thought I'd negotiate later on with him on why all was totally different than he had expected. I then *did get* the fed ex invite within days, *I did go* for the first round of the interviews, and *I did get* accepted after the first grueling round to return for *the gang bang round of ten interviewers.*

At that juncture though, I did come to realize that *he was right,* and they simply want to use me as a marketing guy, *as they do with all they take*, as I've got the supposed *right act* to pull it all off with.... I tried to maneuver quickly during the group bang, and steer the conversation toward portfolio and asset management as well as development, but I surmised quite quickly that this was not going to happen.

What I now know to be categorized as a *valid moment* surfaced, and I knew my B School real estate head was *dead on right.... I was never, and could never be a wh—e.* There are other words that *rhyme with 'more'*, that I am perfectly happy being categorized as, *but this will never be one of them....* And, *case in point*, when I see the global scandals that house is involved in today, with the US government all over them and their unending arrogance....

So I returned to *school* to be taught by the *completely confirmed master who knew me far, far better than I knew myself,* and I went on to accept an offer from a grouping of many offers, at what *we both agreed would be* a *pre-eminent global insurance company/real estate finance house*, and a solid shop to launch my new, *amended* and progressing career.... So after graduation, my tangential/progressive/outrageous/unique/creative and one of a kind career moves on into the permanent lending arena of the larger scale mega deals.... and once again, *I am back in...*

New York, again, after the brief hiatus outside for B School. I had maintained my apartment during the educational sojourn, and had actually sublet it for a substantial amount above what I had been paying... Guess that was my first real estate deal.

Anyway, *life* at the top tier *life company*, initially proved to be exactly what I and others had envisioned. The *right deals* coming across my desk, from the *right institutions and borrowers*, and of the *right quality*. I really had *begun to arrive* at this point *in New York...* I maintained my very strong faith all during this period as always, and was quite thankful for the transition from my previous, more fledgling, *but maybe, then again, no, i.e. fledgling,* career development. A bit of a change of guard though began to emerge at this *previously rather conservative* institution, coupled with a change of *game* plan to a more *brokerage oriented mind set,* and once again I found myself in a state of flux as to *where I really did belong.* I sure *did know though,* exactly where it was that *I did not belong.* Had I naively become involved with an organization that *was evolving* into a *third rate* wirehouse version of where I had previously interviewed that was at least in the top, *first rate* category? One would no longer *perhaps* be judged on deal quality, but *perhaps* on deal volume and size. It *perhaps became* all about bonuses based on such. *Do the math,* and think about *what one may have to think of doing* in order to achieve a top standing and monetary remuneration there... So, *onward, and fast...* this time to a construction lender/developer hybrid containing one of the sharpest financial minds ever.... *oops,* another set of financial *issues* then surfaces here *maybe* related to appraisal terminology, and *onward again into the sunset to seek the promised land....*

Could you even imagine where I would be if God

had not been in my life, and if I had not true faith that somehow this would all work itself out.... Then OK, to *a perceived paradise* where I knew the proprietor for years, and a dream top management position transpires in national real estate development across a wide range of sectors. *The days start* also in a Caribbean paradise, where I learn that the firm is composed of mostly *exceedingly beautiful women*, one of whom is one of my closest friends to this day, and although *quite beautiful and a former Miss* --------, she was quite, *quite different from* ..... Some of the other *ladies* who had some, como se dice, *questionable ethics*.... And on this Caribbean escapade, I experienced *sensations* ranging from *I can't believe this --------- is going on*, to *I knew it could be like this!*

What happened in N----u, stays in N---Hey, I'm an American male, *misguided* at times by American culture, but hopefully on my way to true paradise at one point later on....*And so the days,* and *the years* go on, and the *exposure*, .i.e. real estate development, finance, design, etc. is unreal.... And the genre of carrying out the work in private planes, as well as on more pedestrian jaunts on

MGM Air to *LA*, and on *cigarettes,* of the boating kind in the Hamptons, did appeal to this composite American male quite well I *really honestly must admit*, but *only at times of the five percent category....*

Maybe that whole episode was the garden of good and evil, of pleasure and pain, all intertwined... who *of us* knows... *But, LOVED, LOVED this **GIN GAME**..... kind of La Dolce Vita meets La Vida Loca in all aspects one may care to imagine. Anyway,* incredible projects especially one in particular, that occupied much of my time over this period.... Sophisticated, sensual, cutting edge *New Urbanism*, resort community in *the right* bordering beyond suburban, beyond Stepford Wives *community......* And *the beat goes on*, as my life does also......

And now my own project research, and my now-realized travel desires, took me with the increasing monetary remuneration to such '*in*' watering holes as Sardinia's Costa Smeralda, Santorini's Ia, and Mallorca's Deja, in addition to the more *pedestrian* St Tropez, Capri, St Barths and Cadaques. Yeah, Rome, Athens and Barcelona in there also. . . but again, I am more into *natural flawless beauty landscape,* and *through my own admission then and now*, also into wanting to see *the so-called best. . . .* And *sometimes it is,* and *sometimes it is not*, as *sometimes* it is *genuine beauty* and *sometimes* it is just *perceived glamour. . . .*But one gets exposed, and one learns, and if one has one's head on one's shoulders correctly, and if one has faith and is filled with the Holy Spirit, *one may discern all*, and *keep* and *partake* and *continue only* in the *right arenas... But, I do, do value exposure*, and I *got it,* at this evolving series of apexes that just got better and better....

Until one hits a bit of a crash and then goes into the cave, into a reflective state for a while in order to sort it all out. *And so it was*, and so it does occur, and so one goes through emotions of exuberance, and sorrow, and regret, and melancholy, and thoughts of the good times *and if they really were,* and hope, and despair, and hope, and hope, and depression, and joy, and hope, and **hope**, *and* **hope**, and, and, **and..., and then**, life opens up again, and *outrageous* opportunities surface, and fall, and resurface, and fall, and re-emerge, and get better, and better, ***and better***, and more frequently, and *more intensely*, and ***more*** *vivaciously* and *more realistically, let's not forget*, and the whole situation all merges and *jells...* all comes *into play* and the *right thing* **surfaces** and *there you are...* So from an **implosion** to a *new beginning and fortunately now again... in...*

New York, and now at a major global financial services house where I am Head of Global Real Estate.... Not bad for *after the Fall,* so to speak, of that former.... And living in New York and Toronto, and heading the real estate end of a major merger, and *disagreeing again* on the acquisition number by just a wee bit of 000,000,000's....*Did I imagine that....* and the formation of one of the most incredible business relationships/ friendships, etc. I have had or ever will have... *Now not that that had not been turbulent also...* as it had... but it is back again, and more solid than ever before....and he backed me up **then** which meant everything, and when he went on, *I went on also,* and on to the next, and another top position this time giving me real Latin American exposure, as I always wanted and *secretively* prayed for, and then another merger, and another group of *interesting people of the third-rate kind*, and an outrageous *bigger* than *bigger* trading floor, and first of its kind, and more *interesting people of the third-rate kind* emerging , and then his blow up and then my waiting game, and then the breakthrough and *we meet again*, and on to the most incredible hands-on, lone wolf position where my typical assignment was: Lars, go *to Caracas, figure it all out,* get your people, get a business plan together, get it all written up and get it out for approval, and hire the rest of them; develop it, design it, select and furnish the artwork and accessorize it, and make it worthy of our top, top clients as they need banking privacy worthy of their sublimely understated and discreet demeanor, as we are the right firm, and please do let us know when the place is finished, and get the party started, and tell us when to arrive....

Got it, great, *do it... and so I did*, and *happily/ thankfully* over and over and over and over again, and my life *evolved/devolved* into George Clooney's *Up in the Air* movie, in basically *all ways depicted there*, but with *far, far better location shots*, and with a *far, far better place to call home,* the *right discreet* pre-war Candela *co-op,* on the *right discreet enclave*, in *the right area*, with the *right people*, and later inclusion on the *right board,* meeting and *interviewing* all *the right other people* for inclusion....

Yes, I wanted *the beauty*, and that *really was the point that led to the acquisition*, but then there is also that other five percent that then *occasionally surfaces,* and there is a little of *I want it* because it's hard to get also... *but thankfully not much,* and I am *always grateful*, and I still had/have my faith...*and then* the *trips are wilder* and wilder, and more and more to the range of beyond two weeks a month to three on the road, and it's Rio, Nassau, the Caymans and Panama and BA and Punta del Este, *and back* and *then have to do* Beverly Hills, and Miami and Vancouver and Frisco, but then later let's discuss all in Zurich and London. *And wow*, you are really, really doing great, and *that one* sets *the standard* for *all future ones* from now on, and please do, do continue on, *and on and on and on....* *And on, and on, and on....*

And the location shots where I vacationed, became more and more *out of the ordinary* also, with jaunts to Bequia, Elba, Sperlonga, Na Xamena, Tobago, Formentera, and Lugano taking place in the same *casual manner* that I used when planning a trip visiting friends in Santa Monica. *But, LOVED, LOVED this* **GIN GAME**…. again, *kind of La Dolce Vita meets La Vida Loca in all aspects one may care to imagine…. And, let's just say*, what happened in ------, stays in ------!

But I did maintain my grounding wire and my devotion of God, and I was OK, but *I was a bit involved in all this*, and I did have to remind myself *more and more and more…* of reality, *and what is really important….* Times spent in prayer and meditation in such great European Cathedrals as Grossmünster and la Cathedral de Palma were especially significant *and beautiful* and grounding. And I found myself visiting these incredible houses of worship for *long, long* periods of time whenever I frequented those locales, which was rather frequent. True, *valid moments*, existed here….

And then there is that recurring flashback of 1995, *of what am I really doing,* that occurred after the last big *Gin Game implosion*, and what about that, *then sought after,* back to a Catholic life experience at that undergrad institution, and what about *Peace courses* at night for *a typical weeknight*, etc., etc., *and what if that had happened,* and *what if you had then found it,* etc., etc., etc.

And so here we are again, now in the S*ummer of '06,* and the video tape *replays itself over and over and over,* but on *the slow, slower and slowest speeds possible,* but it *is there,* and perhaps *this is the incredible valid moment that really sets the stage for all to come after...* yes, I think it *is/was/whatever.... It began then..* maybe in a *quasi-denial stage...* OK, *LET'S SLOW DOWN, REFLECT AND ANALYZE....* Good time to play Mary J. Blige, *No More Drama* , and *after that,* let's go to Michael W. Smith*, Place in this World. Wow,* am I writing this or is there some other entity/force/Spirit in play here... I think we are both here, the Holy Spirit and I, and just the way I would like it in my new enhanced, *God-centered life... I/We are here....*

To just complete the thought of *why the pivot point in the Summer of '06, let's just say that a series of things started happening concurrently,* that made me *realize change was in the air.* I remember reclining in a lounge chair on a Mallorcan *cala's* cliff over the sea, and thinking that all was *not to continue this way,* nor was I sure if I wanted *it to continue this way….*

Was I *simply running* and *constantly seeking diversions*? Was I *engaged* in *stalling reflection* on what it was that I *was really supposed to be doing with my life?* Still cannot explain that feeling, *but it was there then*, and I remember it now well….

It was, I now know, *a valid moment of the MAJOR kind…. And I* often have had these deep, *more pensive experiences,* when in such *flawless, natural surroundings…. A valid moment can be truly dazzling.* I have begun to express here certain feelings I have had at times when I have been to certain parts of the Mediterranean in beautiful, natural surroundings. I have had feelings of *having been there already*, and of another place and time, and *not necessarily in the past….* Feelings of crystalline vibrating body composition in play, and possibility of transport…. Total peace and quietude. Calm, serene, air bound/weightless, *at union with….*

At that Summer '06 time, in addition to seeking *moments like this*, I was looking for a second home on that island, as I had been thinking of retiring there *one day….* So I looked, and went through the motions, *but something just was not right....* And it depressed me, *but fortunately/unfortunately, for only just a bit,* to think that this was really *not going to come to pass* for whatever reason.... And there were countless reasons why previously envisioned things might not transpire, as so much was predicated *right then* on my present position of that moment, in an organization that was again beginning to change for the worse.

A questionable South American acquisition of a rather arrogant firm had been bothering me, as it was one that would not welcome intervention and change... No problem with them, but big problems with mothership, as a major sign of weakness was evident in my book, suggesting lack of control and desperation. Constant reorgs had been/were in the works and plagued the company, and I questioned the longevity *of that world* in which I had come to flourish. Also constant global, *como se dice, privacy* changes that could/were affecting the way business was executed, were beginning to appear in *shark feeding* formation, and not in isolated circumstances.

A confirmation of some of the feelings I had had was then to occur six months later, when *again reclining on a lounge chair* poolside at

Christmastime at my sister's second home in the Caribbean, a reorg change would affect me dramatically, although I was confident I would be able to *rubberband* it until I got back to Manhattan. I did, but the organizational structure was changing into something once again that would border a third-rate wirehouse act, and this was not what I had signed up for.

I became *disillusioned* and began to ponder where I might go next. I never attained the answer, and questioned whether I had *played out my GIN hand* in the real estate and building areas and was ready *for a totally different experience.*

The absurdity became increasingly pronounced, and more outrageous things began to happen that were historically completely uncharacteristic of the firm. My position also started changing for the worse *again*, and the quality and strength associated with it for creating a good, solid product began to fall significantly. The firm could indeed not harness the acquisitions and top executives it had attained, and poor standards from other places began to permeate throughout the organization into Europe itself.

I no longer reported to the people I had greatly respected there, and the former CEO left also. Ethics, honest behavior and strong backbone I reaffirmed and thankfully were so key to me, but these qualities were no longer in place in my opinion. *One by one,* the global and national scandals surfaced, and the layoffs, and the inquisitions, and the wolf-pack attacks, and finally *the fear* set in all around.... Finally in the summer of '08, my layoff occurred in about round seventeen, and I entered a period of reflection and further shock as the worsening global conditions unfolded.

This period was an especially rough one, and I found more and more that I would not want to continue on the path I had been traveling. I now especially resented the lack of fulfillment and lack of work enjoyment and lack of pride in work, the lack of altruistic people I had recently been working with, etc. and had no real sincerity when applying for the real estate management positions that surfaced. I also noticed some strange "coincidences" occurring, that I began to feel were happening to help make me realize a few things about paths I thought I had wanted at times in the past, and at that present day.

The first occurred immediately before leaving, when I met a real estate developer/marketer who was focusing on the Las Terrenas area of the north coast of the Dominican Republic. This was an area I had followed for a decade and had just visited finally in March. He and I got to know each other quite well, and shortly before the layoff, we began to discuss an employment opportunity with him. At first I thought this was incredible, and in further dialogue realized it was not the answer to my restless spirit as I was then able to realize that re-positioning my life there was not really what I wanted, nor was promoting the product. It was simply another fantasy one may have when stressed out and thinking about living in a so-called paradise environment. Fortunately it was in my hands, and became of little interest so I did not pursue further.

Then almost immediately thereafter, a major resort developer I had met the year before, that I was discussing employment opportunities with, re-approached me about what first appeared to be a great position again in the Caribbean, with other great opportunities possible in the future all over the Caribbean and Mediterranean. Frightening, as this had been a dream of mine for quite a long time and that I had felt would be impossible to realize. But it did. But again, something was terribly wrong. By mid-October I was actually quite depressed about my path, future, world conditions, feelings of entrapment into what I did not want, and I began to have desires for a whole different life, now strengthening dramatically and intensely at times in a back and forth pattern.

Something with communal living, a Catholic atmosphere, the elderly, people to help, and far more meaning was needed and required for me to continue in life. I questioned if money was the issue and feelings of inadequacy for future field progression, and quickly found that was not it. I realized that even with more than ample supplies of both if given, a whole real sense of purpose was needed as otherwise I would just be hanging around meandering, and I guess in a hold pattern for eventual death. Quite depressing.

By early November, I had the offer letter in my hands for the resort development position, and found I could not complete the signing of it, nor leave for there the following week to commence the undertaking. *Here was a strong feeling of foreclosing on something else that needed to start soon*. Again, I could not target exactly what this was though, but I prayed to God to show me the path, as this "nowhere land" phase I was in, where I could not determine my focus and path, was really bringing me down and depression was clearly there.

At this point I immediately went to see my parish priest in New York. When seeing him, I stated that I knew I needed to come to see him somehow and that I had completely lost my path. I mentioned a feeling about Catholic communal living and somehow helping hard-working people. I said I wondered how I had come here and was I desperate or something and crashing and seeking some kind of security landing. I also said I wondered if some kind of calling was occurring although I had no idea where it was leading.

Father immediately said that it was clearly good that I was there, and both he and I knew I was in the right place and for the right reasons. He mentioned that he had not seen a case like this over these trying times, and others may have gone in downward directions when I chose not to, and knew to come to the Church for counsel. Following my theme, he gave me some material on Catholic life communities, and we decided to speak further after I reviewed it in more detail.

Upon reviewing these materials, I somehow felt nothing in them was strong enough. I began intuitively researching Catholic Worker housing and learning of Dorothy Day. This was feeling better, but again, there was something more I should be doing. I discussed the whole thing further with a friend, Joe, whom I have known for twenty-five years and with whom I had done undergrad Alumni Schools Committee recruitment in the New York area since 1981. He had just been ordained a deacon in the summer of 2007, and he also mentioned the Franciscans that he knew well. He said that he would pray for me, and that I would find the path soon that God wanted for me and where I would find happiness.

Through Joe, and after going through the website of the Franciscan Friars of the Renewal which attracted me, I spoke with a Franciscan priest , and reviewed my feelings to date and what I was going through. Father felt strongly that the paper pushing days of my life were clearly over, that I indeed had a calling, and we would hopefully learn soon what it was exactly. Again following my theme, he gave me websites to explore: L'Arche, Madonna House, and the Catholic Underground. The first two sites were also of interest to me and I respected the theme and work of the groups a great deal. Certainly I saw the need in today's world and was thrilled that they existed. I went to the Catholic Underground the first Saturday in December, and enjoyed the Mass immensely. The rock music part felt a bit off for me, but somehow I was on the right track even though none of the three groups felt like the place I was supposed to be.

Then I had an impulse to go on to the Archdiocese of New York website, and found the NYPriest.com vocation area. While New York did not feel right as to where I was to remain, the points given for discernment as well as where to go from there, did feel right. I then contacted a priest through the site, who mentioned the three seminaries in the United States that took older men. He said that New York would not be in the running because of my age, which was fine as I knew I was to be somewhere else. Only the hills of Rockland County were of some interest, but again, something was off.

When reviewing seminaries over the internet, I initially felt that a different one would be the best overall fit. When learning more of the dioceses connected with each, none really popped out to me but the ones of the Pacific Northwest were of interest. I then decided on another approach which was to reverse the process and start with where my heart seemed to be sending me on dioceses, and the people that I could be associated with living in the parishes. Two areas came up quite easily as my top two choices. I knew both areas and liked them immensely, knowing I would feel at home at either one.

Interest was expressed from both dioceses and I quickly learned that both were connected with another seminary I had reviewed briefly. I then contacted the rector, had a great conversation, and made plans to visit the seminary and stay over. I also learned that this one might be a better fit for me than the other based on the diversity of ages and the strong international element. The visit was great, felt comfortable and right, and arrangements were also put in place to visit with the two dioceses in the coming weeks.

Throughout this process, then followed by further

time of discernment, I have constantly wondered why the feeling of a calling has occurred during this mid-point in life as opposed to earlier. I have also wondered about my education and professional experience to date and have wondered how it would fit. In addition, I wondered about life experiences, past and present relationships, lifestyle, wants, restless spirit feelings, etc. and have sought to make some sense of everything, though realizing I certainly do not have all the answers at this point.

Again there is a strong feeling of working with the elderly in a community as well as something about Church architecture and protection of assets. I came to realize that the latter, of course, certainly works well with my architectural and real estate skills, and the former might have not come to pass unless several life experiences and times of reflection had occurred.

When proceeding with life reviews all throughout my life and especially over this period, the burning question has been "Why have I never felt settled?" There has always been this feeling that I was supposed to be doing something, although I have never been able to figure out exactly what that was.

And at times, I did absolutely feel I was on the right path and in the right place, but again there was a sense of unease that it was only temporary until some final plateau and sense of the "real thing" came to pass. And that sense of the "real" has never occurred in any of my tangential professions in the architectural and real estate arenas, and I do mean arenas as that is how they have felt.

I do not feel that a calling for the priesthood had occurred in the past, although something was happening around 1995–1996 with the desire to return to my old undergrad institution to work there and somehow be involved with the overall community. Again, I prayed that something would open there but it never did transpire. I also had felt it would have been incredible to be able to live tangential lives to see how it might have worked out if something did open up there and what in due time would have transpired.

As previously mentioned, I have always loved quietly sitting in great churches and cathedrals throughout the world, and the recent past years have been especially strong on this feeling. In September of 2007, I specifically set aside a day to go to Iona in Scotland, and loved the time at the abbey. Strong feelings as said also existed at Grossmünster, Salisbury Cathedral, and the Cathedral de Palma. Travel to Europe has always been so key for me, and I enjoy time there immensely, especially, time in some of the older and even newer Churches. The feeling of contentment is strong in many churches especially. All throughout my life I have sought solitude and reflection in them. I also, as mentioned, achieve this on long walks through beautiful areas. The architectural background helps me to appreciate the times there even more. *This feeling of peace and contentment I guess has been a component part of a calling,* and today the desire for more time in Church grows as well as the solitude for reflection. I find enjoyment here. Readings recommended from discernment material have also been great and I continue to seek more at this point.

This is such a contrast also to Fall '08, when strong feelings of depression existed before this spiritual enhancement strengthened. I knew the former path was no longer of interest, nor did I want to spend my time worrying and focusing on my financial future that now required hourly watches of the markets and the absurdity and realization that the average person's life savings were in the hands of market opportunists, day traders, and short sellers. The worsening global conditions made me realize how meaningless all of this was. Did I really wish to spend future days paralyzed, watching this with a constant uneasy stomach and short term plans, or was there something far more important that I should be doing? The economic upheaval was a clear turning point as well as the job offer in the Caribbean that was also loaded with constant short term fluctuations.

I wanted to seek direction and decisions from inside that gave me peace, and my former path and its side streets did not provide this at all and in fact, all appeared dead-end and meaningless. It's not that I felt above everything, it's just that there was something else I knew I should be doing. These other things were best for others. I was happy, though, to know that I am no longer one of them, and never really was actually, if I really want to dwell deeply into life review. But some foundation material had been attained there and I am happy about it; it will be part of the basis for what I will do next.

All continues to this day to point to the Church. The idea of the priesthood evolved from the initial feelings of seeking inclusion somehow more strongly within its sectors. There was a strong feeling that developed mid-part of discernment that a role as a lay person was not strong enough. Perhaps it is also about all that I would learn at the seminary and how God could then place me to achieve my fullest potential. I was so interested in the material I saw in the catalogs. Learning more of God and His will, and all that I have not comprehended to date could be developed.

Reviewing my attributes, God-given talents, inner yearnings, etc. has helped me speculate to a limited extent only on why God is calling me to the priesthood. To date, my own aspirations and goals and what I had settled for have been truly underwhelming compared to what could lie ahead if I were on the correct forward path. I now pray for what God wants for me, where I believe true happiness and fulfillment will also exist.

In the past I prayed many times for what I thought I wanted, and many times, even when wishes were granted, the overall result was something less than what I thought it was, and brought neither contentment nor real joy. I feel God may want to utilize my gifts far more effectively and for a greater group of people than I ever envisioned, with an overall effect of a great combined purpose. Perhaps within the priesthood, these gifts can be utilized best within an appointed parish or within the archdiocese somehow itself or combined in some way. The skills are rather unique, and I also tend to be a quite enthusiastic and cheerful person when on the right path.

Another interesting point about me that has evidenced itself all throughout my life is my need for passion and enthusiasm in my work. This has always been essential to me, and I sought to leave places when it was no longer there and felt it would not be in the future. I have a great promotion and sales personality, but choose not to use it in that manner for anything I do not believe in a thousand percent. Others have noticed this trait also, and tried to capitalize on it, but in the long run, nothing will work unless I am totally on board. I was up for a major position I did not want in the fall of 2008, and the main hiring manager reported back to the recruiter that he would hire me in a minute, but strongly sensed I would never do anything I did not believe in. I considered this a great compliment and he was quite right.

However, in the Church, this passion could be an incredible attribute, and could be quite a strong asset for the Church in its work. When motivated and enthused, I can really be on fire and quite effective in promoting a cause. Interestingly in the past, several have said I would make a great minister, as I had a strong sense of ethics and "the right thing to do." I have also been told that I come across that way quite well without being a self-serving salesman. God may indeed have a purpose for this in the priesthood somehow I feel.

I have also always have had an interest in a simple life, although I wished each of the components and each of the few possessions to be of high quality. Early on I knew that possessions may possess you, and I have tried to be careful. Even today I feel the Manhattan co-op I own partially possesses me as I seek to answer the call to the priesthood. However, I may have figured out how it might help others including a family member and a friend over the long run, and perhaps that is why I still own it. I also know that I am not to exhibit anxiety over it, and God will work it all out in the right time frame. Therefore, I should not stress about it as well as any other possessions, perceived lifestyle needs, and creature comforts, etc. as well as any other dilemmas at this time.

I also feel there are many life experiences I have had that God may want to use as I share them with others. For instance, I have had wonderful educational opportunities that I can share. My experiences in corporate life and decisions I made daily relating to *right and wrong* would provide for an interesting dialogue. Watching my mom age and watching her sense of meaning and purpose weaken as she grew older has also been instructive and is an experience that I can use in many areas. I have had encounters with nature and beauty, especially as they manifest in art and architecture, and have been revealed through my travels, that I still want to share with others. I have had many strong, healthy friendships, some with women (they have always been non-sexual) that I would like to see continue. I also think others might benefit from understanding the discouraging times, how and why situations changed and what finally helped me triumph over them.

 I try to be a very enthusiastic person for the most part and this may be utilized well by God with my overall demeanor and image each day. Also I have been looked upon quite frequently as a counselor to others, even though at times I have no understanding as to why. I do see some good attributes though when I pursue things quietly, and really think them out, as opposed to when acting without proper self-reflection and inner peace with a decision.

Priesthood to me means an opportunity to help others as best as I can and with the newly learned knowledge attained so far at the seminary. The priest is a representative on earth of God's will and a being truly aspiring to be more like Christ each day. A priest sets an example, especially with his peace of mind, which he attains by being on the chosen vocational path, promoting the Church and its doctrines to others, and strengthening their love of God each day.

Also he is a person in which a parish can find confidence. He is a person people can go to with any issue as I did when I felt I had lost my path.

He needs to be a calm and confident leader, and someone who can interface well with other leaders of a community. He truly needs to be a part of the community and maintain honest and genuine care of the place and its people, in good times as well as in bad times. A priest should seek constantly to strengthen the faith of his parish and help them especially with their faith in times of need. He needs to help them in their problems as best as possible and help refer them to others as needed. He is a general clearing house for spiritual as well as general guidance who can help clear the path so others can continue on their God-inspired true vocational paths. His prayer for others is key as well as his true understanding of their real issues and roadblocks.

A priest is also the giver of the Mass and the Sacraments. He is there in times of joy for baptism as well as for marriage, and in times of grief such as at sickbeds and funerals. He is there for confession and for conference to parish members. Priesthood is a strong, multi-disciplined vocation of the highest order, and it is about placing others first and attaining the true genuine joy created when giving.

Fast forwarding a bit, I am now in a seminary. The two dioceses both came in positive, and through Adoration and discussions with great people, I came to know with which one I should align. Also, *turns out* I am a *double vocation*, and in addition to the pastoral route, will also be engaged in chancery work in the real estate, design, investment, and asset management areas. I seek to comprehend and follow God's will to the utmost, and pray that I have the tools, the talents as well as the capabilities to carry out my vocation in the fullest manner possible....

Epilogue

Fast forwarding, without seeking God's constant *inherent* association, is not what I am all about, nor what I have any interest in *devolving* toward. Life, for me, is a joint undertaking between my perceived interests, aims and passions, in conjunction with the guidance from the Holy Spirit. I incessantly seek to find my exact place in this world, along with the appropriate path to follow each day that God has planned for me, which is a constant invigorating, *at times draining, but dynamic*, and quite fulfilling endeavor. I am also not an arrogant being, believing that I have all of the answers, all of the time, leading to all of the right pursuits.

My story continues along in one of the most vivacious ways possible, *and made possible I believe*, by the actions of the Holy Spirit. Others far more versed than I in vocational discernment, have also affirmed a bit of an altered path surfacing in me, and have also encouraged me to *run with it*, if you will, and to follow the intrinsic inclinations, as it indeed appears to be Spirit driven. *At this moment in time* in the Spring of 2012, exactly two years later from the period in time during which *Gin Game Interrupted* was first written, I now find myself firmly interwoven within one of the most wondrous, perplexing and stimulating life interludes imaginable, as I set aside this bit of time when asked to write this brief epilogue to my ongoing, *and ever unraveling,* journey. You see, I have now entered a rather hectic, soul searching, and vibrant life phase where my inner being is seeking a rather dynamic *integration* of the best of my past educational and professional life experiences and God given talents, for inclusion within a new venture extending the Church's mission in Catholic social teaching. My two solid years of seminary formation, have helped further introduce me to a new world of expanded possibilities where my vocation has evolved into a dual role comprised of continuing my Catholic education and formation in the permanent diaconate program, coupled with pursuits in the Catholic social teaching areas utilizing my background in the finance, capital procurement and building areas. Present work at the Archdiocese spans areas ranging from grant attainment for several groups, to premises revitalization, to World Youth Day co-ordination of unified sub groups for next year's program in Rio de Janeiro. In addition, I am now in the embryonic stages of forming a social conscious real estate alternative investment fund that will transform under-utilized Church properties into vibrant, new developments within use parameters exemplifying the statutes inherent within Catholic social teaching. I feel great, *invigorated* and happy to meet the ongoing challenges of each and every day as I seek to carry out my ever-expanding goals and responsibilities.

What has transpired is truly nothing less than absolutely incredible. Case in point on what can happen when you seek God's hand and involvement in your life work *each and every day*. When asked last year how I felt, *as this transitional phase was in the process of developing*, I confidently answered in a split second that I was a *'calm wreck'*. The two wise clergy members, who had asked, then looked at each other and exhibited a subtle, *but quite striking*, expression of contentment on their faces that I *couldn't not*, always aspire to remember. The translation, *inwardly*, was quite *evident*, if one *chooses and seeks* to open up to it. The *wreck* part is easy to comprehend, i.e. a major life change was being internally induced that could be perceived by the *un-aided* eye to be a significant upheaval. To those *who believe* though, the *calm* part is the more simple to comprehend. It is just simply the Holy Spirit affirming that all is *just fine*.

That's really *all the signage* that I will *ever need*, to continue on…

Ordained to be our Priest

Father God,
come lead Your son
to the altar of sacrifice.

He,
the Isaac,
who understands, obeys,
lays down his life.

Yet, unlike Abraham,
You, Father,
sing and dance,
as you bring your new son;

for the Lamb
has already been slain,
and the follower has come,
not to be immolated,
but to celebrate…

and in your space and time:
no population problem,
no limit to those of us who will be saved,
to the generations that will be blessed!

Ronda Chervin

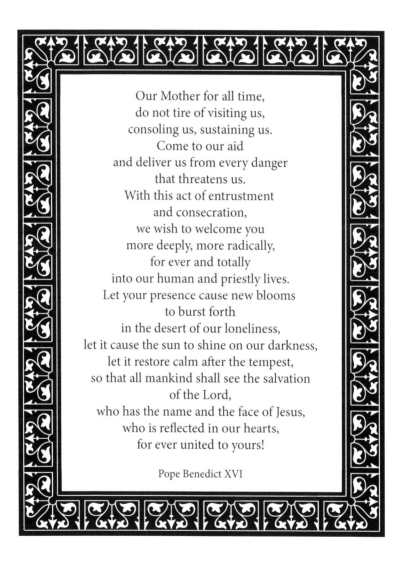

Our Mother for all time,
do not tire of visiting us,
consoling us, sustaining us.
Come to our aid
and deliver us from every danger
that threatens us.
With this act of entrustment
and consecration,
we wish to welcome you
more deeply, more radically,
for ever and totally
into our human and priestly lives.
Let your presence cause new blooms
to burst forth
in the desert of our loneliness,
let it cause the sun to shine on our darkness,
let it restore calm after the tempest,
so that all mankind shall see the salvation
of the Lord,
who has the name and the face of Jesus,
who is reflected in our hearts,
for ever united to yours!

Pope Benedict XVI

On My Journey
to the **Priesthood**

A Son of God

This seminarian is in a religious order and wishes to remain anonymous. His journey reflects a faithful, disciplined servant who nonetheless took many years to hear the call to the priesthood. But ultimately, and only in God's time, he did hear himself called by name.

When Saint Luke wrote his Gospel almost two millennia ago, he portrayed Our Lord Jesus Christ as a merciful Messiah who came into the world to reveal the loving face of God. May this short essay exemplify for contemporary souls that eternal and unshakable mercy of God.

Before starting to write about my path towards the priesthood and the meaning that it has for me, I would like to give some historical information about myself. I was born in a country in the Southern Hemisphere in 1961, at a time when local agriculture was flourishing. My parents were practicing Catholics — married in the Church around 1957 — and dedicated to assuring that their four sons were well-instructed and good students. From this early experience came responsibility in meeting our duties, self-discipline, education, and a light but constant awareness of the existence of God.

My father was a businessman who studied accounting. Sadly, he left our home in about 1968 and divorced my mother. He then started a new family with his current wife with whom he has five children, four boys and a girl.

My mother was a professional nurse and worked all her life in the Ministry of Health and Social Assistance of my country. About seven years after the divorce, she moved out from our house and married a radiologist, with whom she had no children. I have good relationships with my parents and all my brothers.

Even with good religious formation throughout my life, I have struggled to understand God's call to me. This seems to be a common situation throughout the ages. If we look at the Holy Scriptures, we will find several examples of people struggling to understand God's call to them.

Let us consider the story of the call of Samuel (1 Samuel 3:1-10). Samuel was a young boy serving in the temple when he heard, on three different occasions, a voice calling his name. He assumed this voice was that of the priest Eli. Eventually, Eli realized that Samuel was hearing God's voice calling to him and instructed him to respond, "Speak, Lord, for your servant is listening." Samuel needed Eli to tell him that the voice he heard was God's. He didn't recognize God's voice on his own.

Similarly, I have been called by God on several occasions in the depth of my heart to be a priest. I want to refer only to three of them. The first time was about 1967, when I was a six-year-old boy who desired to love God and to inspire others also to love Him. One of my aunts asked me in front of the pastor of my parish if I wanted to be a priest like him. I responded affirmatively. Although I was a pious child with great devotion to the Sacred Heart of Jesus and the Child Jesus, I was not aware of what being a priest really meant.

I went to Christ the King School in my town for my elementary, middle, and high school studies from 1967 to 1978. The school is owned and administered by the Order of Clerks Regular, founded by Saint Joseph of Calasanz. By the time I was in high school, I was an assiduous attendant at the charismatic meetings at my parish. I learned there to be devoted to the Holy Spirit, the Virgin Mary, Saint Joseph, and to read the Bible every day. Since that time, anything related to religion and the Church has been of interest to me.

I graduated from high school in July, 1978, and immediately went on to study electronic engineering at the university level. It was in 1979 when I met members of Opus Dei for the first time and I became a member Numerario.

The second time I was told that I should be a priest was in 1981, during my vacation from school and the study of engineering. The pastor of my parish told me, while I was praying before the Blessed Sacrament, that I would be a good priest. In those days I was a member of Opus Dei, receiving a good and vast religious education through their study program. I had in mind to go for the priesthood once

I had finished my studies of electronic engineering. Unfortunately, the vocation to Opus Dei was not for me, so I left in 1986.

After receiving my bachelor's degree in 1985, I was hired by a telecommunications company to work in the satellite division. This job opened the door to an intensive period of training, participation in international telecommunications meetings, and a considerable growth in my professional skills and knowledge. I represented and defended the interests of my country and other countries' employers in various telecommunications meetings in Argentina (1988), Cuba (1989), Peru (1993 and 1994), Venezuela (1994), and México (1995).

These experiences gave me great satisfaction as well as the opportunity to grow professionally in many aspects. It was very challenging to convince people from different parts of the world and with different mentalities about the success that would come from adopting my point of view. There were difficult negotiations in the development of satellite communications which resulted in good business deals and furthered the goals of my employers. With this success, came a greater sense of personal fulfillment.

In 1988, I was part of the delegation of my country that participated, with another 2,000 delegates from all over the world, in the World Radio-Communication Conference. In 1995 I attended the International Telecommunication Union (ITU of the United Nations) that took place in Geneva, Switzerland.

It was in 1989 that the German government granted me a scholarship to study telecommunications in Germany. I lived and studied there between 1989 and 1992, followed by five months in the United Kingdom. My interest in operatic, symphonic music and in theater deepened. These experiences enlarged my heart in trying to live and deal with very different people, many with opinions completely opposite to mine.

Once I returned to my country, I started working with a telecommunications company again while studying in the evenings for a master's in theology (1994-1995) at a Catholic university.

In the midst of so much professional success and personal development, I also experienced a certain amount of physical suffering. In 1994, I was operated on and my spleen was removed. Since then, I have suffered from myelofibrosis, also called thrombocythemia, which is a blood disorder. Even today, I need prescribed medicine to control my platelet count. Later on, I developed allergies to various foods, including: nuts, soy, shellfish, chocolate, alcohol, carrots and beans.

Between 1994 and 1995, I was hired by a group of countries to protect their interests and advocate for their plans in satellite communication at international meetings and also to defend the interests of my country before the Inter-American Telecommunication Commission which is a body of the Organization of American States (OAS of the United Nations). It was in 1995 that I met some managers of an American satellite operator—the largest satellite operator of the world—headquartered in Washington, D.C., and they offered me a position to work in the international telecommunications department along with the option of pursuing a master's degree in business administration (MBA) at George Washington University. I decided to move to the United States in 1996. I worked at Intelsat from 1996 to 2006, receiving my MBA in May of 2003.

When I came from Venezuela to the United States my spiritual life became more contemplative. My interest in the priesthood was aroused in the year 2001 and my spiritual director at the time told me I had a vocation to the priesthood. He prepared the soil of my soul for the third call that happened in 2003. In that year I had the blessing of meeting a very holy soul who was to me what the priest Eli was to Samuel. With his then fifty-two years of fidelity and dedication, he taught and inspired me to respond to God with,"Speak, Lord, for your servant is listening." Previously, I had learned from my many good spiritual directors how to stand before the Lord. With this holy priest, I learned, like Samuel, how to listen and receive the Lord's words.

It is this act of listening, combined with prayers, penance and the guidance of the Holy Spirit through my spiritual director, that led me to the awareness of my contemplative and priestly vocation and deepened my love for Jesus, our Eternal High Priest. Like Saint Peter, I want to answer "yes" to Jesus' question, Do you love me? It is a "yes" expressed with all the strength of my soul and the desire to be a victim with Christ on the Cross for my own sanctification and the salvation of souls.

During all this time, up to the third call, my religious life had become organized. Mass every day, daily Rosary and Angelus, reading the Bible and spiritual books, Confession once a week, one hour of Eucharistic Adoration each day; these were among the religious practices I had kept from the time of being a member of Opus Dei.

From about 1981 I also strove to do works of mercy. Most of them were done under the guidance and encouragement of the good spiritual directors that I have had in the last twenty-seven years. Briefly, I was able to offer a specific spiritual work of mercy by instructing others in the Faith. I taught the catechism to fifty children who were preparing for First Communion. This experience, of seeing pure souls who desired to receive the Lord, gave me much satisfaction. All of them received the Most Precious Body and Blood of Christ. Additionally, I had the opportunity of teaching courses for teenagers who had joined the army. I gave about eight talks, one per week, regarding drug addiction and how God can satisfy the souls of the young people. This experience was very fulfilling because I strove to present to them the great adventure that it is to follow Christ.

I also held sessions with young adult and senior parishioners in reading the Bible, explaining the basic truths of our Faith, and how to read a spiritual book. I encouraged them to seek personal holiness, be apostolic, and practice works of mercy. I had great satisfaction when two ladies who used to attend those religion classes decided to become nuns. I also explained to friends the teachings of the Catholic Church. It was like a personal apostolate. Some friends went to Confession after many years away from that sacrament and others returned to the Catholic Church.

Providing good counsel to others has long been part of my apostolic activities. I have done this always with any person (relatives and friends mainly) who asks and is open to receiving my advice, especially if it is about God. Always wanting to convey that loving and trusting God is the solution for any difficulty, I have had many opportunities for advising, consoling and comforting others.

Since Christ was and is my hero and model, forgiving was one of those qualities that I emphasized most in my life. I have always tried to forgive others because Our Lord Jesus Christ says blessed are the merciful — they will receive mercy. Not least among the spiritual works of mercy, bearing wrongs patiently has enriched and improved my spiritual life greatly.

As a lay person I participated in the corporal works of mercy as much as possible. Feeding the hungry was a beautiful experience. I volunteered to take care of about ten elderly people, who lived unattended in an abandoned house. After a few weeks, the Sisters of the Poor received them into their nursing home and attended to their needs. The best service that the Sisters provided was bringing them to religious practices and preparing them to go to heaven.

Clothing the naked and visiting the sick cultivated a good desire for helping others. Making donations of both money and food to the poor through the parish also granted many opportunities for exercising corporal works of mercy. I had the delightful experience of being a volunteer, preparing food (peeling potatoes mainly) with the Missionaries of Charity and taking care of elderly people in the Sisters' facilities in Washington, D.C. Elsewhere, sheltering friends who were in great need was one of the most touching experiences I have had in my life. The practice of spiritual and physical deeds of mercy helped me to savor the goodness of God and moved my heart to put the Gospel of Our Lord Jesus Christ into action.

Because the priest partakes in the priesthood of Christ, he is a living and transparent image of Christ the Priest; thus he is called to fulfill the ministry of the Good Shepherd who seeks the lost sheep, and of the good Samaritan who binds up wounds. He takes the place of the father who awaits the prodigal son and welcomes him home upon return, and of the judge whose judgment is both just and merciful. By administering the sacraments to souls, the priest is the sign and the instrument of God's merciful love for the sinner.

It is my understanding that the priestly vocation is given by the Lord Jesus Himself. It is a call which is as personal and individual as His calling the twelve apostles by name or His calling of the prophet Jeremiah. It is a call to service of others for the sake of kingdom of heaven. It is this communion of purpose and of action that makes the priest one with Jesus the Eternal High Priest and with one another, just as Jesus and his Father are one. So, the priest is a sign of unity, the unity of the Most Blessed Trinity. Thus, priesthood is not merely a task which has been assigned or a profession to be exercised; it is a vocation, a call to be heard individually again and again.

In the Gospel of St. Mark the priestly call of the twelve apostles is graphically displayed. "Jesus went up the mountain and summoned the men he himself had decided on, who came and joined him. He named twelve as his companions whom he would send to preach the good news. . ." The passage in Mark 3:13-14 then lists the names of the twelve. Here, I can see three important elements of the priestly call given by Jesus himself that I think are present in my vocation. First, Jesus called his first priests individually and by name; so Jesus called me by name, drawing me to a deeper spiritual life and apostolic zeal through the advice of holy friends and spiritual directors. Second, Jesus called the apostles for the service of his word, to preach the Gospel; I strove always to live according to the Gospel and therefore to preach by the example of my life, in addition to the religious education classes I offered to children, teenagers and adults. Third, Jesus made them his own companions, drawing them into that unity of life and action which he shares with his Father in the very life of the Trinity. The spirituality of my contemplative vocation is both incarnational and trinitarian, with a strong emphasis on living the mysteries of Christ.

Following the example of Jesus, the Eternal High Priest and Divine Master, the priest is asked to make the entire gift of himself, to lay down his whole life as a sign of his great love for the Lord and his flock. This is not something imposed from without on the person offering himself for the priesthood. It flows naturally from all that it means to be a priest as someone who signifies and shares in a very special way the ministry of the Good Shepherd himself. A priest is asked at his ordination to make three special promises: celibacy, obedience, and simplicity of lifestyle. In my case as a contemplative in a religious community, I am asked to make a public profession of the evangelical counsels of poverty, chastity, and obedience.

For any single Catholic layman thinking seriously about the priesthood, there is no doubt that it is not an easy decision to make. Many truly generous-hearted and dedicated people still find it difficult to make a lifelong commitment to all that the priesthood involves. This is especially true of the celibate way of loving that is asked of the priest, and the aloneness this sometimes brings. Marriage and family life are among the greatest human joys and blessings. I had many good opportunities to marry and have a nice wife. However, because I have always longed for God, even in the years I was not consciously aware of it, I felt more inclined to celibacy. It was not a deliberate decision, but I was greatly attracted to it. In other words, I enjoyed more having a heart completely dedicated to God than splitting my heart with God and another human person.

Handing over the freedom to plan one's future in the promise of obedience to the religious authority can also be a real sacrifice. The priestly ministry calls for a poverty of spirit, which involves not only a simple lifestyle, but also the loving surrender of much of one's time and privacy. Most people see obedience as something that takes away our freedom, limiting our ability to decide for ourselves the course of our lives. For the priest, it means the opposite. Like celibacy, it is an expression of love for the Lord whom the priest has freely chosen to make the sole meaning and purpose of his life. Jesus was the obedient one;

His whole life was surrendered in love to the will of His Father. The priest is asked to live out in his own life the obedience of His Lord. He makes his own the words of Jesus: "My will is to do the will of the one who sent me, and to complete his work." (John 4:34)

Is this asking too much? Not for the man whose ministry will be to make visible among people the undivided heart of Our Lord Himself. Like a couple at their wedding, the priest freely and joyfully gives himself to his Lord and the Church, "for better, for worse; for richer, for poorer; in sickness and in health; to love and to cherish," for the rest of his life. Like marriage, priesthood is a lifetime commitment. It calls for a radical giving of one's time, and of all that one has and is.

At ordination, the prostration on the ground is a powerful symbol of the spirituality asked of the priest throughout his ministry. It is that of the suffering servant whose life is given for God's people. He resembles the Good Shepherd who becomes the Lamb of God, laying down his life for the flock.

As I write this essay and reflect on what it means to be a priest, I feel unworthy, unsuited, and apprehensive about all it will involve. This is natural, so I shouldn't worry about it. No one is ever worthy of the priesthood. The apostles themselves were a very mixed crowd, with their own weaknesses and doubts. I often echo Simon Peter's words to Jesus as I sense Jesus calling me to some special service: "Leave me, Lord; I am a sinful man." (Luke 5: 8) But Jesus called Peter all the same. What matters is not how I feel, but that Christ is calling me. But how can an ordinary man, with all his weaknesses and failings, be a living image of Jesus Christ as high Priest and shepherd of his Church?

All ministry is the free gift of God who delights in choosing the weak to be servants of His presence. It is not for me to ask, Why me? God chooses whom He wishes. I am not chosen because I am better than others, or more worthy than they. Like God's people in the Old Testament, we are special because we have been chosen, not chosen because we are special! The priest is no less in need of salvation, forgiveness, and healing than any other disciple. It is the Holy Spirit who unites the priest to Jesus Christ in a special way at his ordination, and the priest is totally dependent throughout his ministry on the continual outpouring of the Spirit of God. A priest is a man of God's pardon, an instrument of forgiveness to others, but he is also a sinner, in need of forgiveness and renewal himself. Therefore, a priest needs to be a man of humility, realizing that in his weakness the Lord calls him to do wonderful things, and that he does these things, not on his own merits, but through the power of God working in him.

In spite of his fragile nature, the priest, a servant of Christ, is placed not only in the Church but also in the forefront of the Church, to stand with Jesus for the truth of the Gospel and the teachings of Mother Church. This highly demanding duty reveals that the vocation to the priesthood, with its corresponding commitment to celibacy, is a precious gift of divine grace. With undivided heart, the priest follows Jesus, the Good Shepherd, in an apostolic communion, in the service of the people of God. The holocaust of his entire being to God for His glory and the salvation of souls, then, is to be welcomed and continually renewed with a free and loving decision. His entire being expresses the priest's service to the Church in and with the Lord Jesus, the Eternal High Priest in the order of Melchizedek.

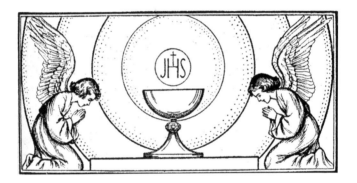

Priest of the Word

Did you once dream,
my priest,
of fiery sermons,
for a flock of saints?

When, then, do you feel now,
my priest,
when you look out at your
patiently enduring sheep

who
endure everything—
the Word?
the homily?

Your face tells me
that you trust
the long endurance:
wives of husbands,
husbands of wives;
workers of bosses,
bosses of workers;
brothers of sisters,
sisters of brothers –

Trust endurance
as a good yet unripe seed;
the fruit –
we shall eat together
in another pasture,
in perfect joy.

Ronda Chervin

181

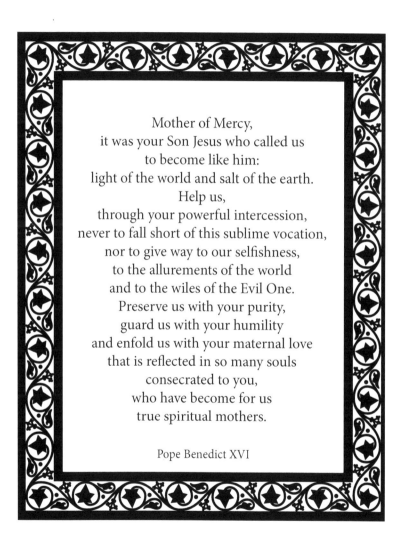

Mother of Mercy,
it was your Son Jesus who called us
to become like him:
light of the world and salt of the earth.
Help us,
through your powerful intercession,
never to fall short of this sublime vocation,
nor to give way to our selfishness,
to the allurements of the world
and to the wiles of the Evil One.
Preserve us with your purity,
guard us with your humility
and enfold us with your maternal love
that is reflected in so many souls
consecrated to you,
who have become for us
true spiritual mothers.

Pope Benedict XVI

183

# With God All Things Are Possible!

Rev. Bradley Pierce, M.S.A.

Father Bradley Pierce captures an essential of many priestly vocations, namely, not to stop the movement forward, but rather, if God has a different plan, let the Church place the roadblock. Don't place it there yourself. God gave this life to you and knows best how to use it.

My faith life began at a Baptist Sunday school. It was a beautiful experience because I met a very loving and merciful Jesus. However, this belief didn't last very long, maybe four years, and certainly not long enough to receive baptism, which took place in our Baptist church at about ten years of age.

Even after those four years, faith and God didn't have a central place in my life. To be honest, I'd have to say that God didn't have any place in my life. After my conversion, one of the things that struck me was how many Good Fridays I had lived through without being aware of them, nor being conscious of the incredibly loving event they commemorated.

My life was a pursuit of the enjoyable things of this world. I never had a sense of sin apart from hurting people or being dishonest. I failed to finish high school because of one course I didn't bother to complete. I spent what would have been graduation night near the ocean at a sorority cottage. I wasn't bothered at all about not graduating.

Soon I enlisted in the army and ended up in the Eleventh Airborne Division of Fort Campbell, Kentucky. I passed the GED exam for my high school diploma and entered Columbia University when I got out of the service.

While at Columbia I worked nights at the Stork Club, which was New York's most fashionable night club in the 1930s, 40s and 50s. I thought this was a wonderful way to make a living, so after two years at Columbia I left school and went into the night club business full-time.

The clubs that I managed or owned from 1956 to 1974 were filled with celebrities, from the Beatles and The Rolling Stones to Frank Sinatra and Judy Garland. My lifestyle, like many of my customers, was that of sex, drugs, and rock and roll.

Religion was not part of my life during these years. In fact I had lost faith in the reality of God. There was no religion but there was a spirituality. I was not in the club business for the snob appeal of the café society and celebrity clubs. I ran the night clubs to make people feel loved and feel special. I trained my employees to do the same and not to make Frank Sinatra feel any more special than the biggest nobody that might come into our club. I never questioned what a person did or what they thought. I loved and respected everyone, including the heads of two mafia crime families. I got more love and respect from them than I would have ever gotten from many people in the church pews.

When I came into the faith I realized I had already begun to live the spiritual life because I had always loved human beings the way Jesus tells us to love them. Jesus teaches us to love everyone as God loves us, without condition. And "everyone" includes our enemies, those who hate us, those who curse us, and those who hurt us.

Our Lord Jesus had this to say to Sister Mary of the Trinity about how we should love everyone and make them feel special:

"A true mother will not consider her child ugly, no matter how much it may be so. To her it is always lovely, and so it will always remain in her innermost heart. That is precisely the way My Heart feels towards souls, though they be ugly, soiled, filthy. My love considers them always beautiful. I suffer when their ugliness is confirmed to Me; on the other hand, I rejoice when, in conformity with My parental sentiments, someone dissuades Me about their ugliness and tells Me that it is not true and that they are still beautiful. The souls are Mine, for them I have given all My Blood.

"Now do you understand how much My parental Heart is wounded by every severe judgment, reprimand, or condemnation, even though based on truth, and how much comfort, on the other hand, is afforded Me by every act of compassion, indulgence and mercy? You must never judge anyone, never say a harsh word against anyone; instead, console My Heart, distract Me from my sorrow; with eager charity make Me see only the good side of the guilty soul. I will believe you, and then I will hear your prayer in her favor and will grant it. If you only knew how I suffer when I must dispense justice! You see, My Heart needs to be comforted; it wishes to dispense mercy, not justice!"

I was "spiritual" but not religious. I didn't have the religion to teach me about God and His plan for us. But because I was loving people unconditionally, God loved them through me, and I was receiving God back from them. Jesus said to Sister Josepha Menendez, a 20th century Spanish mystic:

"Love Me in others. Even if you don't see me there, love Me there anyway and you will bring Me out of them."

"I cherish each soul with a tenderness of which your human love has no conception. Do you not understand that? They must be loved for My sake. Strive to make it known to all whom I put in your path."

"It is impossible for you to know the value and the virtue of others, but you will never have too great a respect for souls, because I have redeemed them all at the price of My Blood."

"Your neighbor is always I, I who am asking of you or giving to you. The Holy Trinity is there in his soul. And if It has been driven out by sin, help your neighbor to receive It back by treating him as if I were already dwelling in him." Quotations from Sister Josepha Menendez can be found in Words of Love (Chicago: Tan Books, 1985), a compilation of writings of 20th century mystics.

After my conversion, I would realize that living the spiritual life consisted in loving all who were put in my path, and by having this habit already, I experienced much of His peace, joy and love during the earlier period of my life.

We all have God within us. God is present from the time of our creation or we would not exist. God is existence and apart from Him nothing can exist. That's why when Moses asks God, "Whom shall I say sent me?" God said, "Tell them I Am Who Am."(Exodus: 3:14) God is present in all human beings. If He weren't, we would disappear like a puff of smoke.

(Note from Dr. Ronda Chervin: the following two paragraphs could be easily misinterpreted. Most Catholic theologians I have read interpret the words in the Mass about Christ partaking in our humanity that we might partake of His divinity not to mean literal divinization but participation.)

The purpose of my life journey is to bring God to life in us and in the world by prayer and love so that one day we will be divinized and become gods as the Catechism of the Catholic Church teaches. (CCC #460)

We need to practice a religion in order to learn how to achieve this transformation. We can be spiritual when we love and find peace, joy and happiness, but to be "divinized" and be fully transformed into God, and made perfect as our heavenly Father is perfect, we need Jesus Christ to teach us about love and goodness and how to live in harmony with God. We will enter the kingdom of goodness and love and live the divine tranquility and bliss forever only with His help.

During this earlier period of my life I had lost faith in God. That faith was restored by my friendship with a gangster who came into the club that, ironically, I had named Salvation. I was told that growing up, he was one of the two toughest guys in Brooklyn. When he would come into my club with a couple of other guys, I knew he might be a little scary to the other customers. So I would try to hide him a little, making him think I was giving him special seating. I saw something good in him that I liked, but I was not sure if he was a sociopath or not.

One night he said to me: "After I leave here I realize you put me over here, you put me over there. No one tells me what to do. We're going in your office (he takes his gun out and puts it on my desk), and either we are coming outta here friends, or only one of us is coming outta here." Despite the threat, I liked him enough to want to be friends, and that is what we became.

Some years later I had an epiphany. One day I said to myself about my friend: How can something packaged so ugly have something so beautiful inside? Instantly I realized the reality of a soul and God in that soul. From that day on, I never doubted the existence of God.

Even though I now believed in a loving God, I didn't have the structure of religion to tell me how I needed to live to express my love and gratitude to God. Even when I was sinning, not knowing that I was doing wrong, I thought God was happy because I was happy.

Then one day, in 1974, when I was thirty-eight years old, I had a grace to recognize that I was sinning. I immediately got on my knees and asked God to forgive me. I never doubted His forgiveness because I had met the loving and merciful Jesus in Baptist Sunday school.

We should never doubt God's love or mercy when we have humbled ourselves by repentance. Jesus tells us that God is more hurt by our lack of confidence in His love and mercy than by our sins which come from weakness. Listen to His words to Sister Josepha Menendez:

"I pursue sinners as justice pursues criminals. But justice seeks them in order to punish; I, in order to forgive."

"I want them all (souls) to have confidence in My mercy, to accept all from My clemency, and never to doubt My readiness to forgive. I am God, but a God of love! I am a Father, but a Father full of compassion and never harsh. My heart is infinitely holy but also infinitely wise, and knowing human frailty and infirmity, stoops to poor sinners with infinite mercy."

"I love those who after a first fall come to Me for pardon. I love them still more when they beg pardon for their second sin, and should this happen again, I do not say a million times, but a million, million times, I still love them and pardon them, and I wish to wash in My Blood their last as fully as their first sin."

"Never shall I weary of repentant sinners, nor cease from hoping for their return, and the greater their distress, the greater My welcome. Does a father love a sick child with special affection? Are not his care and solicitude greater? So is the tenderness and compassion of My heart more abundant for sinners than for the just." (Words of Love, p. 60)

Our Lord said to St. Faustina that the greatest sinner has the greatest right to His mercy. Why? Because they need it the most. For all eternity no human or angel will ever plumb the depths of His mercy. It is fathomless.

At the moment of my conversion I was not only graced to recognize my sins, but also to realize that all the roads I and so many people have walked in the search for happiness—including pleasures, material things, successful careers, fame, and even marriage—are not the roads that lead to happiness. There was only one road left and that road was the way of Truth and the life of happiness we seek, found in Jesus Christ.

I told Jesus that I would follow Him on this road wherever He led me, ready to give up my lifestyle and my night club business, spending the rest of my life seeking Him. Jesus responded to me in an inner voice saying, If you will find Me anywhere, you will find Me most powerfully in the Eucharist. Up until this point, I had been to a Catholic Mass no more than ten times. When I was very young I would go with a friend to his Catholic church instead of going to the Baptist church. After about five visits I fell off the kneeler and made a big noise and never went back. Later in life I went to Mass a few times when I was dating a Catholic girl.

Even though I had attended Mass only a few times I must have recognized something powerful taking place at the Consecration because I knew what Jesus was saying. I knew the Eucharist was the presence of God. I also knew that communion in my Baptist church was only grape juice supplied by the pastor's wife.

I said to myself, When I was a sinner I went all the way. Now that I am going to follow Christ I want to go all the way and receive all the gifts Christ left to His Church. I would have to find a Catholic Church that was giving instructions.

After going to a couple of churches, a priest told me St. Patrick's was offering instruction in the Faith and I went through the program. I was baptized and received First Communion and Confirmation during Holy Week, in Our Lady's Chapel at St. Patrick's Cathedral in New York City, on April 9, 1974.

I wanted to spend my first Easter someplace special. I had a friend who told me about a place he had gone one Easter where the monks chanted a beautiful Easter Vigil. I spent my first Easter at St. Joseph's Abbey in Spencer, Massachusetts.

While there, I took a tour of the abbey given by the monks, and I saw a fellow dressed in a different habit than the other monks. He was one of three men who were not thinking of becoming monks, but who were invited to live the Cistercian life for three to six months. I immediately thought that this was what I needed for a total behavior modification.

I expressed my interest, and the monks invited me to visit several times over the next six months to see if I had the mental stability to go from a night club existence to a monastery where the monks live in silence and spend many hours in prayer each day.

I was accepted. On All Saints' Day, I closed my night club at four in the morning and gave it to a friend. I entered St. Joseph's Abbey the next afternoon. The six months I spent there were among the most beautiful I've spent in the Faith. In this atmosphere of silence and prayer, God's presence is so thick as to be palpable. The touch of God's love and peace I felt in my heart was amazing.

While at Spencer I discovered two things that influenced where I would spend the second six months of this amazing first year in the Faith. I listened to a cassette tape by Patty Gallagher. It related her experience of the beginning of the Charismatic Renewal at Duquesne University. Two priests gave a retreat weekend on the Holy Spirit to some Catholic students at Duquesne. The priests had previously gone to a Pentecostal church where they received a baptism in the Holy Spirit.

This idea of the "Spirit" was new to Catholics who only knew the Holy Ghost (as the Holy Spirit was then called), and for most Catholic lay people It was a ghost. (Note from Dr. Ronda Chervin: in the sense that they rarely thought of the Holy Ghost as a personal being.) Gallagher related the powerful experience of the Holy Spirit that she and her fellow retreatants had. I felt I had already received the Holy Spirit at my conversion, but to be sure I went for three months to the Word of God Charismatic Community in Ann Arbor, Michigan, to attend a Life in the Spirit Seminar. All the big wigs of the charismatic movement, Ralph Martin, Steve Clark, Jim Cavnar, and Bert Ghezzi prayed over me, but nothing special happened. Yet, the prayer meeting that followed was very beautiful.

The next day I went to Mass in the evening. I

was supposed to meet someone after Mass; but when I received Communion, a peace came over me that was so strong I couldn't get up to leave. I was in a state of peaceful bliss until I dragged myself out of my seat about a half hour later because my friend was waiting for me. The Holy Spirit had given me my special experience in the Eucharist, that which brought me to the Catholic faith.

While at St. Joseph's Abbey I also learned about a monastery in the south of India that was founded by a Cistercian priest from Belgium. This monastery was established in the style of a Hindu ashram where one sat in the lotus position to pray the Liturgy of the Hours and Mass. Before becoming Catholic I had had some beautiful spiritual experiences with two Hindu mystics. I decided to go to this monastery in India with the intention of spending the rest of my life sitting at the feet of God.

The monastery was on top of a high mountain opposite the mountain where St. Thomas is reputed to be buried. The experience there was very beautiful. Often at times of prayer we could see clouds beneath us out the cloister windows. Even so, less than ten minutes after my arrival I knew that this particular monastery wasn't going to be my vocation.

Since I had traveled all the way to India I thought I should visit the sister that I had heard so much about, Mother Teresa. So I struck out from the southwest of India to the northeast. When I arrived in Calcutta I took a rickshaw-bicycle taxi to Mother Teresa's convent and knocked on the door. The sisters took me in their ambulance to the House of the Dying, where the sisters bring the people they pick up off the streets of Calcutta to give them an experience of God's love before they die.

I worked in the House of the Dying and stayed in the house of the Missionary of Charity Brothers until a nun invited me to join her in her ministry, a center for those who have leprosy. I lived and worked there for the rest of my stay in India with a priest from Blessed Damien's Community, Father Petrie. He asked me if I ever thought of becoming a priest. I told him I wanted to give myself totally to God in a religious vocation, but as someone small like Brother Francis of Assisi.

He said: "You can't do that. Even though you were wasting God's time, God wasn't wasting your time. God was developing gifts in you and you need to offer these gifts to God to use as He wills. And, besides, the priest is supposed to be the smallest person in the Church, the last and the servant of all."

I replied: "I want to serve God as He wills. I don't know if He is calling me to priesthood. I just know I want to give myself totally to God and marriage or some career will not be enough to satisfy. So I'll just walk in the direction of priesthood and put the burden on God either to open or close that door."

One of the ministries I have had at Holy Apostles Seminary, where I still work, has been admissions. I often talk to men who feel they might have a calling to the priesthood. I always tell them to pursue the priesthood. You keep walking in that direction, and don't stop yourself. Let God stop you through the Church. Otherwise you will be a very unhappy person if you find out at the end of your life that God was offering this wonderful and privileged gift of priesthood and you didn't accept it. Age shouldn't be a barrier. At Holy Apostles Seminary we have prepared many excellent priests who came to the seminary when they were over forty.

When I returned from India to my parents' home in Connecticut, I didn't have to do any searching for where to begin my journey to the priesthood. Five different times I was told by people and through a magazine article about Holy Apostles Seminary in Cromwell, Connecticut. When you respond to God's call, God will grace your path in extraordinary ways to lead you to the door you are to enter.

I applied, was accepted and joined the community that founded the seminary, the Missionaries of the Holy Apostles.

Since my ordination in 1983, I have worked at the seminary as a member of the priestly formation team helping seminarians prepare for the priesthood by walking with each seminarian, making sure he is taking on the mind and heart of Christ. In general, I don't see my ministry as a priest much differently than my ministry in the night club business! I still see myself ministering God's love and mercy to those I pastor, helping them know how special they are to God. The difference is that now I can do it in the most powerful way, because I have the truth and the sacraments of God's love and mercy to give them— the Holy Eucharist and Confession.

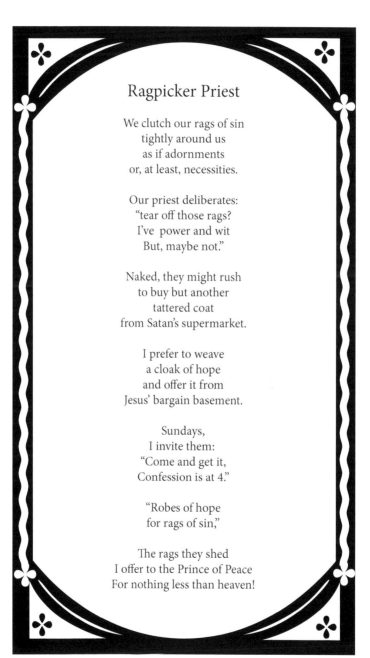

Ragpicker Priest

We clutch our rags of sin
tightly around us
as if adornments
or, at least, necessities.

Our priest deliberates:
"tear off those rags?
I've power and wit
But, maybe not."

Naked, they might rush
to buy but another
tattered coat
from Satan's supermarket.

I prefer to weave
a cloak of hope
and offer it from
Jesus' bargain basement.

Sundays,
I invite them:
"Come and get it,
Confession is at 4."

"Robes of hope
for rags of sin,"

The rags they shed
I offer to the Prince of Peace
For nothing less than heaven!

Ronda Chervin

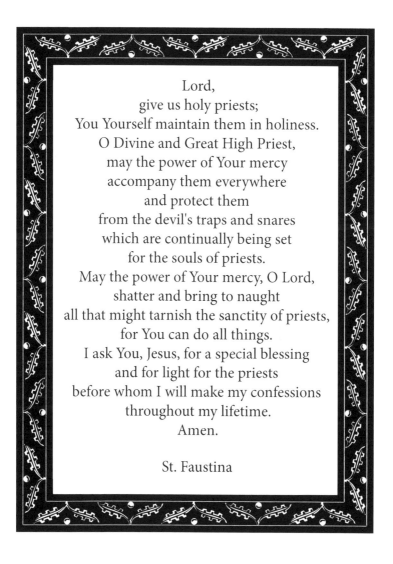

Lord,
give us holy priests;
You Yourself maintain them in holiness.
O Divine and Great High Priest,
may the power of Your mercy
accompany them everywhere
and protect them
from the devil's traps and snares
which are continually being set
for the souls of priests.
May the power of Your mercy, O Lord,
shatter and bring to naught
all that might tarnish the sanctity of priests,
for You can do all things.
I ask You, Jesus, for a special blessing
and for light for the priests
before whom I will make my confessions
throughout my lifetime.
Amen.

St. Faustina

From the Desert to Priesthood

Rev. Deacon Dan Bastarache

Who of us is really worthy of God's infinite love? The answer is none of us and at the same time all of us. Even with our gravest sins manifest for all to see, when we repent, God welcomes us with open arms, even into his priesthood.

I was born in 1952 in the city of St. John, New Brunswick, Canada. My father was a Roman Catholic but he left the Church to marry my mother. She was originally Catholic; but when she was six years old, she had medical problems. As a result, my grandfather approached the priest and asked if he could enroll her in the protestant school that was closer. The priest did not accept this solution, so my grandfather, being a stubborn Highlander of Scotland, pulled the whole family out of the Church and put them into the Baptist Church.

My twin brother and I were raised Baptist and attended Sunday school. I went to church and Sunday school all the way up to the age of seventeen when I entered the armed forces as a medic. Prior to this, at sixteen, I had been set to be baptized. However, I hesitated for reasons that are pertinent to my eventual late call. My grandmother on my father's side used to watch Fulton Sheen on TV. I used to watch, too. I had always wanted to be a priest and a Catholic, and because of this feeling, at sixteen I didn't feel right in my heart about being baptized in the Baptist Church. I chose not to, and of course this was a concern for my family.

In the army I went to church sporadically. Occasionally I would go to the Catholic Church but not participate, except as a spectator. I never participated in Holy Communion in any church because I had not been baptized. That would sometimes make me feel insecure, wondering if others were speculating about why I didn't receive.

At the army base I began to drink heavily; and within a couple of years, I was drinking alcoholically. I was also in and out of many sinful relationships. After serving in the army for eight years, I joined the Canadian Coast Guard and sailed with them for twelve years.

My pattern of sinful relationships continued. Sometimes the woman would want to be married; but I wasn't ready to make a commitment, in part because the alcoholism had weakened me physically, mentally, and spiritually. This weakness affected my self-esteem. I didn't think I could be a good husband or father. To my knowledge none of these women became pregnant, probably because they used contraception.

I always prayed, more so when I had my back to the wall. I would always go to the Catholic church because it was always open, and because the priest was always in the rectory attached to the chapel, whereas protestant pastors lived in married quarters separate from the chapel. I always thought one day I would like to be a Catholic, but I took no steps because of my sinful lifestyle. I would think, *Why would God want me?* I think many people feel that way.

My first exposure to Alcoholics Anonymous (AA) was when I was nineteen, and I went in and out six times by the time I was thirty-one. Right from the beginning, I drank daily, mostly at clubs in the army mess. By the end of my drinking career, I was mostly binge drinking. I thought daily drinking was the problem, and so I would only drink on the weekends. I came to find out that I was putting as much in me on the weekend as I would have done on a daily basis. I am a big man and I could drink twenty-four beers and then get into the whisky.

But with binge drinking my tolerance diminished so that I could get drunk on much less. I didn't pass out. I would function, but have blackouts and not remember what I had done.

When I was thirty-one, I became involved in a common-law marriage with a mother of four children. At the same time my job was on the line because of my drinking. Both the Coast Guard and my companion told me to clean up my act or leave.

So I returned to AA for the seventh time, completely broken, but knowing I had to make some changes in my life. I adopted the Twelve Steps into my life, especially step three, "We made a decision to turn our wills and our lives over to the care of

God as we understood Him." This was very powerful because I always believed in God and was still open to whatever He might want to do with me. I had never gotten as far as the third step in the past because of my fear of God and what He might think of me.

So I got my first six years sobriety on the ship and with the same wife. We talked about marriage on occasion. But then I found my AA program growing in a different direction, and my partner thought I shouldn't continue. She thought that she could save me herself. This mistaken idea is quite common. Recovery isn't about having a savior wife. The spouse should support your efforts to change while you stick to the tried and true Twelve Steps.

After eleven years of sobriety I started going to Matt Talbot Retreats. Matt Talbot was an alcoholic in late nineteenth and early twentieth–century Ireland. He had a spiritual awakening, which eliminated his alcoholism, and then he began to help others. Whereas previously he had spent all his spare time in bars, after his conversion he went every morning before his longshoreman job to 5:30 a.m. Mass. The movement of Matt Talbot Retreats is in honor of this courageous man who now is a candidate for canonization.

The retreats are normally facilitated by recovering priests and nuns! This type of leadership rekindled my thoughts about the priesthood. In 1992, the relationship with my "wife" ended by mutual agreement.

Soon after, I was asked to be a pallbearer at a Catholic funeral. This was the first time I had ever gone to a Catholic funeral; so I was not prepared for what took place. I was also nervous. The priest had a very deep voice that resonated right through me. When he came to bless the casket, some of the holy water fell on my hand and it tingled. I remember looking at the priest who smiled at me, and I got the feeling I should meet this man another time.

When it came to Communion, I stayed in my pew wondering what others were thinking. I could have gone up but my heart told me not to do it because I was not baptized.

On the way out of the church ,we stopped to remove the pall. I lost sight of the priest momentarily. Then I saw him again standing at the back of the church. He smiled at me and bowed, and again I had the feeling I should meet this man.

By this time I had left the coast guard and was working in addiction detoxification for the province of New Brunswick. I felt that in this way I could give back what had been freely given to me by God through AA. Quite a number of people who stay with AA find it is a bridge back to the Church.

I was now in another relationship; and a short time later, I began living with this woman. I decided I needed another round of step four, "We made a fearless moral inventory of ourselves," and step five, "We admitted to God and to ourselves, and another human being the exact nature of our wrongs."

I went to the rectory of the priest that I had seen at the funeral a few months before. I asked him if he had any knowledge of the Twelve Steps and he said, "I may," with a smile. So after he gave me his ideas about the Twelve Steps in general, I realized I had made a good choice. This confidence is very important when you decide to tell your faults to someone. He told me to take my time. I did my fourth and fifth steps, and I came up with about forty-four pages of things I had done wrong and needed to admit!

When it was done, I felt so light and alive, and I explained to him that I had always wanted to become a Catholic. He suggested that I take a year and return to my roots and make sure I didn't belong more to the Baptists. That was a very good move because it brought me back to my rejection of baptism at sixteen. After the year of going back to the Baptist Church, I still felt a void in my heart.

So I went back to the priest and we talked about the RCIA (Rite of Christian Initiation of Adults) process. I started in 1993 and was baptized at the Easter Vigil in 1994. In the process I had to give up my extramarital relationship and live alone for the first time in a long time. At my baptism, for the first time, I felt completely clean inside, totally sin-free. What a feeling!

The ceremony was so humbling. I remember afterwards an elderly lady who was a part of the RCIA group looked at me wearing the alb and said, "Someday. . . ."

I replied, "Oh, please, one day at a time." But I knew that the idea of priesthood was still there.

In 1997 I slipped on a rubber mat covered with snow and ruptured both quadriceps tendons. I had two surgeries on my legs. Three weeks later I went home, but it was too early and the tendons ripped again. I was told I might never walk again, and if I had a blood clot, I would die. I continually asked God for the courage to do what I had to do; and lo and behold, nine months later I went back to work full steam. This incident gave me great trust later in every time of crisis. In hindsight, I think this was the start of my last call to the priesthood.

I continued working in addiction care, and then, in 2001, I started working with adolescents. I had a another brief relationship with a woman. I lived in a small village where there wasn't daily Mass, but I would go as often as I could during the week and on Saturday or Sunday.

In 2004 I really got a stronger calling. I felt it many times, but I kept pushing it away. Finally I approached a friend of mine and asked who would be a good priest for me to consult about this call. Without hesitation he said, "Father Peter." I had been to this retired priest's Masses, but didn't really know him. Part of the discernment included doubts because of feeling unworthy. But eventually the sense of unworthiness became a positive part of my discernment.

After spending about a year and a half meeting once a week with me, Fr. Peter felt there was possibly a call taking place. So I approached the vocation director of the diocese, Fr. Doug, and I went through the procedures. I sold all that I had and gave it away to the poor.

By August of 2006 I was on my way to the United States to Holy Apostles College and Seminary in Cromwell, Connecticut. I hadn't been in a classroom since my early twenties; so coming to the seminary at fifty-four was quite a shock, to say the least. I have had much help from the faculty and fellow seminarians, all brothers I have bonded with — a mix of some older, some younger, some from Canada, some from the United States, and some from other countries.

I have found that the Twelve Steps have given me a certain depth of spirituality that I can give to others when needed. I hope to be ordained in 2011.

(Note from Dr. Ronda Chervin: Fr. Bastarache was ordained June 3, 2011.)

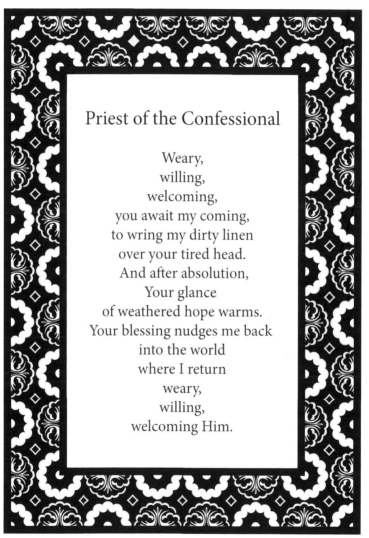

Priest of the Confessional

Weary,
willing,
welcoming,
you await my coming,
to wring my dirty linen
over your tired head.
And after absolution,
Your glance
of weathered hope warms.
Your blessing nudges me back
into the world
where I return
weary,
willing,
welcoming Him.

Ronda Chervin

O Mary, Mother of Jesus Christ and Mother of priests,
accept this title which we bestow on you
to celebrate your motherhood and to contemplate
with you the Priesthood of your Son and of your sons,
O Holy Mother of God.
O Mother of Christ, to the Messiah-Priest
you gave a body of flesh through the anointing
of the Holy Spirit for the salvation
of the poor and the contrite of heart;
guard priests in your heart and in the Church,
O Mother of the Saviour.
O Mother of Faith, you accompanied
to the Temple the Son of Man, the fulfillment
of the promises given to the fathers;
give to the Father for his glory the priests of your Son,
O Ark of the Covenant. O Mother of the Church,
in the midst of the disciples in the Upper Room
you prayed to the Spirit for the new People and their Shepherds;
obtain for the Order of Presbyters
a full measure of gifts, O Queen of the Apostles.
O Mother of Jesus Christ, you were with Him
at the beginning of his life and mission,
you sought the Master among the crowd,
you stood beside him when he was lifted up
from the earth consumed as the one eternal sacrifice
and you had John, your son, near at hand;
accept from the beginning those who have been called,
protect their growth, in their life ministry accompany your sons,
O Mother of Priests.
Amen.

Bl. John Paul II

213

He Brought Me in by the Back Door

Rev. Thomas Simon

Fr. Simon's Aunt Heddy prayed for a priest from within her family for a long time -- not for a week or a month, but over a lifetime. Her faithfulness in prayer, and the faithfulness of Father's parents' prayers also, can be very instructive. God will answer in His own time.

I was born in 1940 in Toledo, Ohio. The birth was unusual in many ways that ultimately affected my childhood and adult life. You see, my mother had been orphaned a few days after her mother gave birth to her. She was raised by her grandparents, and developed an abiding fear of childbirth. After the birth of my older brother she hoped to avoid another pregnancy. She was a nervous wreck whenever she was fertile. This brought about tension with my father. So my conception was a kind of miracle. Then, just before my delivery, the hospitals in Toledo experienced a serious disease in the pediatric wards. Dad's friend, Dr. Andy, chose to come to our home for my birthing.

My father was a pharmacist. He was absent most of the time working twelve to fourteen hour days. He had very little help and covered the whole drug store most of the time as well as filling prescriptions. His parents had run a bar, but by working odd jobs whenever he could, and with their help, he managed to get a higher education.

Because of the atmosphere at home when Dad was a little child he did not trust family the way most of us would. He seldom shared his feelings with us and had little to say unless he was telling a story. He seemed more communicative and friendly with strangers. But I always admired his honesty, frugality, and hard work. I never saw him drunk and he seldom used a bad word.

He was not a hugger or kisser, but he was very faithful. Dad had a genius for building things. Plumbing, electricity, wood working, concrete work and design were all within his grasp. He was also a good baker. After his retirement he became a great gardener and baker and earned blue ribbons and monetary prizes for his pies and cookies. A good person at heart, he lived to be one hundred years old and died during his hundredth birthday party. I anointed him on the spot. What a shock. A massive heart attack took him within seconds.

My mom was a strong, intelligent, good–looking woman. In childhood she led the life of an orphan with her elderly grandparents and did not have the opportunity to go beyond the eighth grade. She went off early in life and became a maid in the home of a wealthy Toledo family. There she got used to being around many different kinds of people and this made her a strong, outgoing person with the best cooking, housekeeping, and entertaining skills. As soon as my brother and I were old enough, she helped Dad at the store, and eventually when Dad sold out, became a top sales person at Lampson Department Store.

All these circumstances affected my character. Even though I was somewhat introverted, like my dad, I could get along with anyone, too.

When I was three years old I nearly died of a breathing attack. Because I was treated immediately, I survived. In another brush with death at the age of eight, I survived nearly drowning in a swimming pool. Then later in the air force, after an operation, I had a pulmonary embolism that almost killed me, too. These brushes with death have made eternity much more important to me than this earthly life!

I grew up in a neighborhood where I was the oldest in my group of playmates. So it fell to me to organize most of our fun in sports, chess, and baseball. I was usually the bad guy in role–playing games like cowboys and Indians because no one else was interested in that part!

Mom and Dad were faithful to the Church. They always went to Sunday Mass. They taught me my prayers and sent me to Catholic school all the way up to and including one year in a Catholic university. However, we never prayed aloud in the house, not even grace before meals, until long after I was ordained a priest.

The first time the priesthood touched my life involved my Aunt Heddy. My mom loved God and later told me that this aunt who was a favorite of ours had prayed all her life that someone in the greater family would have a vocation. She was strong on devotions and probably a daily communicant. All the males in the family that could have answered the call either married or were dead. I was the last one who could answer the call.

As a teenager I had no intention of being a priest, but there had been an incident in fourth grade of significance in this respect. A Sister Regina Marie was teaching the Mass to us and she asked me to play a role by helping build an altar and getting candle sticks, etc. Dad also helped to build the altar during the school year. On the very last day of classes, Sister stopped me in the playground and she asked if I would promise her something. Of course I said yes. "Promise me you will pray for vocations every day." I did this for a long time, and since I prayed the Hail Mary for this intention, Mary was involved with it.

I think God is a bit laid-back. He hides behind the clouds, but somehow He coaxes our hearts along, as long as we have a prayer life and are open to Him. I had lots of hormones and always liked girls. Even though my mom played stick ball and was kind of tomboy, she was very attractive. My older brother never dated. Instead, since Dad told us nothing, he learned about sex when he went in to the navy. He knew nothing about courting and made a poor marriage that lasted for nine years. Then my brother broke with his family. My guess is that in modern times he could have gotten an annulment.

Since Mom and Dad thought my brother had made bad choices, Mom devised a clever plan for me to do better with the girls. She called the mother of my best friend in seventh grade and suggested that the two mothers send the two sons to ballroom–dancing classes. Since we only liked playing ball and had no interest in dancing class, they separated us for two weeks, telling each of us separately that the other one wanted to go to the classes. That is how we found ourselves at the bus stop one freezing Saturday, reunited to go across town to dancing classes.

There we got to know girls and it was fun. In high school, when there were dances, we both knew how to act and it was a wholesome start. Although I dated only a little, I dreamed of having four or five kids someday. I didn't like being in a small family such as mine had been. My brother, being seven years older, had always been jealous of me. With more kids in a family of my own, I thought, there would be more chance for closeness.

I started college at the University of Dayton but left and went to Northrup Institute of Technology in California to study aerospace engineering. I have always loved airplanes. I am gifted in spatial relationships, not books and pen and paper. I always went to Mass every Sunday. During the Vietnam War I had a deferment from military service until six months after graduation as an airframe power–plant technician with a bachelor's degree in aircraft–maintenance engineering. After graduating I decided to join the air force and became a maintenance officer.

I like structure, so I enjoyed the military. For a while, I was stationed in Thailand and saw how the war was being fought. I decided for moral reasons I didn't want to be rotated back to Vietnam. It seemed there was no way to win that war with the Pentagon's not trusting the "in theater" generals and sergeants to make the battle decisions.

During this time I had two appendix–related

crises leading to surgery. Even more than war, my third near–death experience resulted in thinking that sex and girlfriends were secondary to eternity. A sudden death could come at any time.

Also, I was constantly falling in love with girls who were somewhat like my father in being distant emotionally. After twenty-three women I started to get more serious with four but eventually broke up with all of them. God saw to it and I never found the right woman.

When I left the military at around twenty-seven, I went back to Toledo, Ohio, and worked with my mother's brothers building machinery in a tool company. Both my uncles were married but childless, and since they were both over seventy, I was in line to learn the ropes and take over the operation.

It was in choir at church that I met some people who brought me into a much deeper relationship with Jesus. The first group was the Cursillo. With my background of going to Mass but never praying with others, it made a big impression on me that they were like a family in the Church, praying together and discussing their daily lives. I found it so encouraging that I decided to get a spiritual director, Fr. Nicholas Weible, who suggested that I might have a vocation since I was not dating and had broken up with all those women. I also starting going to charismatic prayer meetings. I attended a Life in the Spirit Seminar where I was baptized in the Holy Spirit. It seemed as if the Holy Spirit that I received in Confirmation had been left in a gift box with the ribbon still on it and never opened. When I was prayed over my heart was opened, and I burst into the Catholic faith in a new way.

Two weeks after having been baptized in the Spirit, I decided to hunt for a seminary. I started thinking about the Diocese of Toledo but that didn't work out. An old girlfriend introduced me to a visiting priest, Fr. Zercie of the Missionaries of the Holy Apostles.

Fr. Zercie told me about Holy Apostles Seminary in Connecticut. I shopped around a little but then visited this seminary. Brother Jeff, who answered the phone, was the first one at the seminary that I met. Fr. Ovian was the rector and Fr. Menard, the founder, was still alive and active in the society, frequently visiting at the seminary. I took philosophy courses as a non-sponsored student and heard Fr. Menard talk about the charism of the Missionaries and the priesthood in homilies, at days of recollection, and during retreats.

I worked in the school offices during Friday work periods and I got to know everyone. One day Fr. Bud Raney invited me to go to Peru for two weeks to see their missions even though I couldn't speak Spanish. I prayed about the time and expense, but between money I had saved and help from Mom and Dad I got to go with the General Council members. Br. Jeff and Br. Paul were with us when we visited the various houses and parishes that were near Lima and up in the Andes mountains.

On my return to the United States I made my first promises in the community and everything unfolded. I was amazed that I passed the philosophy courses. At that time they didn't have theology courses at Cromwell, Connecticut. Even though I was not sure I was called to be a priest rather than a brother, God pushed me by His Providence through the back door, as it were, by having me sent to Sacred Heart Seminary in Hales Corners, Wisconsin, a late vocation seminary with a theologate. I got through with a master's in divinity. I was ordained in 1979 on the Feast of the Angels.

Then I began many different ministry posts. I spent a year in Peru with Fr. Menard, but my Spanish still wasn't good enough. So I went to St. Mary's, Petersburg, West Virginia, to do parish work there and at St. Elizabeth Seton in Franklin. I also served at the naval station at Sugar Grove, W. V., and was the visiting priest at Epiphany Church, Moorefield, W.V.

Being the only priest with a parish and mission churches to serve also was very lonely. After six years, I asked to be transferred and was sent to our house of studies in Washington, D.C. There I heard confessions at the Shrine of the Immaculate Conception and became a chaplain with the Christian Brothers.

Later I assisted at St. Augustine's Parish in Elkridge, Maryland, where St. John Neumann was once assigned. I was there for about four years and met the chaplain from St. Agnes Hospital in Baltimore, where I subsequently helped on my off days. Being with the sick, from tiny babies to the very old, including shooting victims and accident victims, too, was very fulfilling.

While I was involved in these ministries, an opportunity arose to open a retreat house in Janesville, Minnesota. Brother Cordoni, Fr. Karempolis, and

I were chosen to go explore this situation which evaporated with the Lord's healing the owners of the property where our prayers and anointing took place. After four months in Minnesota I found myself on the way to Immaculate Conception Church in Waterbury, Connecticut. This new assignment as an associate pastor providentially began on the Feast of the Immaculate Conception and lasted eleven years. During that period the church was consecrated as a basilica. I still serve there from time to time as a visiting priest.

During these years my dad's health deteriorated and required some extra attention, so my superior was kind enough to assign me to the Provincial House at Holy Apostles Seminary. Mom had died at seventy-eight while I was stationed in the Washington area. Dad lived another twenty-two years, during which I discovered, somewhat belatedly, what really great parents I had. Dad died on the Vigil of the Assumption of the Blessed Mother, having attended as he regularly did, the Sunday Mass at Joan of Arc Parish and having said his daily Rosary.

I look back on my parents and thank God for them. I pray God that their lives become even more in eternity than they ever were in this world, while always giving God more glory. I ask in Jesus' name. May God be praised by the work I am still able to do. The past years I have been living in the Cromwell Community Provincial House. My ministry now is in five different local parishes on an as needed basis. I am also a member of the Provincial Council, the acting chaplain of the MSA Mass Association (not the administrator), acting provincial bursar and secretary of the Corporation of the MSA at Cromwell. I serve the provincial when possible.

I praise and thank God for His patience in answering Aunt Heddy's prayers and using his Divine Providence to bring me through the back door into His sanctuary. Actually God didn't have a chance with the Blessed Mother, my mother, Aunt Heddy, Sr. Regina Marie, and St. Therese of the Child Jesus and the "Twenty-four Glory be to the Father Novena." How can I miss this great vocation in service to God and the Church that Jesus founded and sustains through the Holy Spirit in spite of me! I have never regretted becoming a priest. I always felt that God did want me to be a priest.

A special thank you to Br. Steve King, Br. Jeff Hermann, and Fr. Pat D'Alesandro who got me started on the Rosary in the old chapel. I pray for God's blessing and give my deepest appreciation for the patience and kindness of Dr. Ronda Chervin, who is editing this piece with real love and generosity.

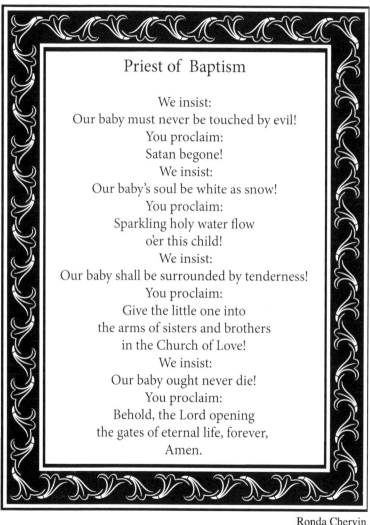

Priest of Baptism

We insist:
Our baby must never be touched by evil!
You proclaim:
Satan begone!
We insist:
Our baby's soul be white as snow!
You proclaim:
Sparkling holy water flow
o'er this child!
We insist:
Our baby shall be surrounded by tenderness!
You proclaim:
Give the little one into
the arms of sisters and brothers
in the Church of Love!
We insist:
Our baby ought never die!
You proclaim:
Behold, the Lord opening
the gates of eternal life, forever,
Amen.

Ronda Chervin

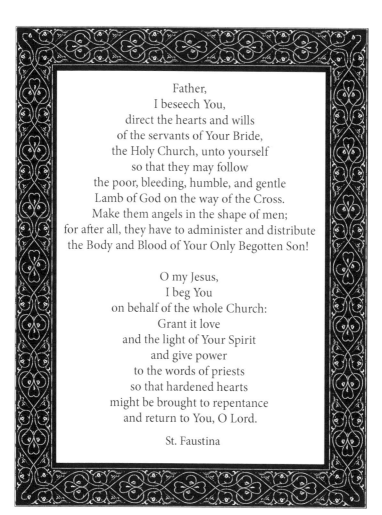

Father,
I beseech You,
direct the hearts and wills
of the servants of Your Bride,
the Holy Church, unto yourself
so that they may follow
the poor, bleeding, humble, and gentle
Lamb of God on the way of the Cross.
Make them angels in the shape of men;
for after all, they have to administer and distribute
the Body and Blood of Your Only Begotten Son!

O my Jesus,
I beg You
on behalf of the whole Church:
Grant it love
and the light of Your Spirit
and give power
to the words of priests
so that hardened hearts
might be brought to repentance
and return to You, O Lord.

St. Faustina

Worshipping at the Source

Guillermo Gabriel-Maisonet

The power of liturgy to transform us is so evident in this piece. We are indeed what we pray.

I was born in Arecibo, Puerto Rico. This is a large city of about 100,000 people but within rural surroundings. I was the first born and only son with two younger sisters. My family was not Catholic but Methodist. My father, a police officer in the tactical operation branch, was not a churchgoer. My mother, however, took us to church frequently, usually every Sunday.

I went to a Christian school run by several churches. English was taught two hours a day. As a kid I always had an interest in religion. I loved singing, which is a big tradition for Methodists. We didn't pray at home together, but I remember when I was eight years old praying hard for the safe birth of my younger sister.

When I was thirteen, Jesus became personal for me. A lot of us go through such a conversion in our early teens. This was when I began to think of the possibility of becoming an ordained minister someday. I was fascinated by the pastors, the preaching, and the worship in church.

At sixteen years old I went through another big spiritual awakening. I was very involved in school with a Christian student movement. That was when I truly knew without doubt that I was called to ministry. For my last two years of high school I went to a public school to study. There I was even more involved with student groups.

These were very spontaneous, not organized by any outside movement. You would have seen in these groups Catholics (eighty-five percent of the population), Methodists, Pentecostals and evangelicals of every sort. The Catholics who went to our group in the public school were mostly charismatic. Girls and boys would do things together but not date in the way they do at such an early age in the United States.

While in high school getting ready for college I decided to study history because I thought that would be good later for seminary. I studied to be a history teacher in the education department. But when I transferred to the main campus of the University of Puerto Rico in San Juan, I became a history major.

During my time at the university I went through a spiritual crisis and I stopped going to church and stopped praying with others. However, I kept on attending campus ministry groups. Part of the difficulty was moving from home to a metropolitan area where I started to experience all that the world had to offer.

Even though I was in this crisis I would still talk to God, and even in my worst times I could not imagine embracing a life totally estranged from God. One of the things that kept me going was that I didn't deceive myself that what I was doing was right. I don't have any respect for people who try to say that sin is okay.

In my Christian ministry group my friends eventually helped me to come back to God again in a more serious way. Soon I became the leader of such a group, and I dated one of the girls who was a member. After my term of leadership, when I was about to end my studies in college, I went again through another spiritual crisis.

During this time I met a philosophy professor who was also a pastor of the Reformed Episcopal Church. (This is a small group that was the first to break off from the mainline Episcopal Church.) I went to see him not because I wanted to become a part of his church but because I needed spiritual direction. He offered it to me but insisted I need to go to church and why not his church?

So I began to attend services. At the beginning I was a little scared. Even though it was in the Anglican tradition, it was quasi-Calvinistic. Methodism is different. But I was fascinated by the liturgy. By the way, the Anglican/Episcopal liturgy is much more reverent and traditional in many ways than the present-day Catholic liturgy.

At the Methodist church there was a liturgy with holy communion once a month. At those times the pastor would wear a chasuble and stole and there was an altar railing. But at the Episcopal church, liturgy was much more prominent. The first time I heard the minister saying, "With angels and archangels and with the whole company of heaven we laud and magnify thy glorious name, ever more praising Thee and saying, Holy, Holy, Holy. . . ." I was fascinated. It was the first time I came to an awareness that through worship we participate in the heavenly worship. It was the first time also that I became conscious of our relationship with the heavenly beings and all those who have departed. I was thrilled that we can be in contact with the Church Triumphant.

Even though it was a mission parish meeting in a rented, non-sacred space, I got the impression that what was happening was much larger than that space; what we were doing was cosmic, transcendent in dimension.

I began to study the doctrines of the Anglican Church by myself and with this pastor. Because he knew my life story he was aware that I was interested in ordained ministry, so when our bishop from America came to visit the parish, I was introduced. The bishop wanted me to study in a new seminary in Louisiana.

So, in the fall I came to the United States for the first time and studied in this seminary. It was a very nice place because there was a benefactor who also ran a company and arranged for the seminarians to work at his business. Our pay was enough for our expenses, and in this way, we finished without debt.

I was there for four years. It was a privileged time. We studied one subject at a time with professors flown in by the benefactor from England, South Africa, Germany, and different parts of the United States.

After four years of theology I was ordained deacon and was sent back to San Juan, Puerto Rico, with the caveat that since my pastor was taking a sabbatical for doctoral studies, I would be the substitute for a mission of about twenty people.

At this time, because they could not support me, I found a job as a librarian at a college and also taught at a local Reformed seminary a few semesters. I dated one of the members of the church.

After two years I resigned my position as a pastor because the denomination disbanded the mission. I began to attend the mainline Episcopal Church in San Juan. During this time I started to have a greater desire to participate more often in the liturgy. The church I was going to had liturgy only on Sundays. I didn't want to go to just any protestant church, but I thought of the Lutheran church. They, also, had liturgy only on Sundays.

The only place I could go to liturgy during the week was the Catholic Church, and there was one just near the house I was renting. I started to go after work every time they had evening Mass and then discovered they had morning Masses, too. I didn't want to become Catholic, but I had a great thirst for worship. That was the reason God created me. By this point I had changed from being a "memorialist" (those who believe holy communion is only a memorial of the supper of the Lord) to a believer in the Real Presence. So Sunday I went to the Episcopal Church and weekdays to the Catholic Church.

By now I was thirty years old. I had broken up with my girlfriend, though we are still friends to this day. Eventually, I thought of entering the mainline

Episcopal Church; but when I further analyzed Anglicanism, I became baffled by what was going on, such as allowing serial marriages and not being strong on life issues. Each local church would have a different moral stance.

I thought that there was no place for me in the Episcopal Church because of the problem of authority. Some of the bishops were heterodox. I decided at this point to study the Catholic Church. For a present my sister gave me The Catechism of the Catholic Church. I began to watch Journey Home on EWTN, and I began to talk to friends who were converts to the Catholic Church.

It took not just study of the doctrines of the Church, but also special graces to lead me to the Church. One time I was reading the Catechism late at night. By 1 a.m. I had reached the Primacy of Peter. When I read the quote from scripture "Thou art Peter and upon this rock I will build my church," (Mt. 16:18) for some reason it was as if I were reading it for the first time.

So I ceased to be protestant, but I still didn't want to be Catholic. It was something visceral. I told God He couldn't make me be Catholic. I considered Catholics to be the lowest type of Christian.

Then I started to read in a systematic way John Henry Cardinal Newman's Development of Christian Doctrine and also the Church Fathers. Eventually I called Journey Home. Through the staff I was put in touch with a convert, an Australian priest living in Puerto Rico. I entered into conversation with him until, finally, I had no good reason not to become a Catholic.

This was 2002. I introduced myself for the first time to the priest where I had been going to daily Mass. He knew that I had been studying the Catechism, and he welcomed me without the usual long RCIA program. So at Easter I was received into the Catholic Church.

I came into the Church because I became convinced that the Church was the one Jesus founded, but I still didn't like the Church. I loved high liturgy, and the Church at this time was more casual than the Episcopal Church. I found it tacky. I recall two times after the Mass when I cried and told God He couldn't force me to put up with this tackiness. I wanted everything to reflect that we are entering the throne room of Jesus, the King of the universe.

Because of this conflict I thought I needed spiritual direction. One day I was watching the local Catholic TV channel, and I saw a priest consecrating the bread and wine. I thought this priest really believes that Christ is in his hands. Not that the other priests I had known didn't believe, but with this one the belief was evident. I called the station, and I found him. He became my spiritual director.

After our second or third meeting, I told him about my life and my desire to be a priest. He said that he didn't think I had this call. I suffered very much, but I made my peace with the idea I would be a layman the rest of my life.

After three years with this priest, he told me that he thought God was calling me to the priesthood now. I laughed, but I have always believed in Providence. God opens doors and closes them, and this certainty gives me peace because then I know that I am doing

His will, not mine.

Now, with the open door, I was introduced by my spiritual director to a Puerto Rican bishop from Tyler, Texas who was visiting in our area. We met, and he invited me to come to his diocese. I was looking to come to the United States in any case for a change.

In less than a year, he sent me to Holy Apostles College and Seminary for studies. Within the next few days of this writing, I will be ordained a transitional deacon. When I become a priest, I plan to celebrate the liturgy with the kind of reverence I have always longed to see.

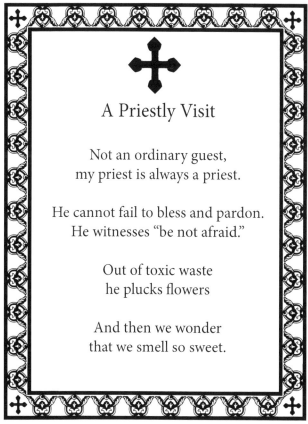

A Priestly Visit

Not an ordinary guest,
my priest is always a priest.

He cannot fail to bless and pardon.
He witnesses "be not afraid."

Out of toxic waste
he plucks flowers

And then we wonder
that we smell so sweet.

Ronda Chervin

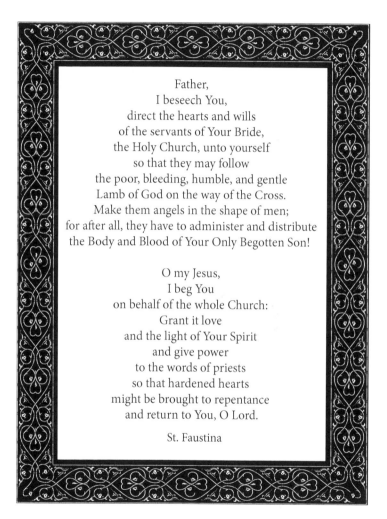

Father,
I beseech You,
direct the hearts and wills
of the servants of Your Bride,
the Holy Church, unto yourself
so that they may follow
the poor, bleeding, humble, and gentle
Lamb of God on the way of the Cross.
Make them angels in the shape of men;
for after all, they have to administer and distribute
the Body and Blood of Your Only Begotten Son!

O my Jesus,
I beg You
on behalf of the whole Church:
Grant it love
and the light of Your Spirit
and give power
to the words of priests
so that hardened hearts
might be brought to repentance
and return to You, O Lord.

St. Faustina

Afraid Not to
Answer the Last Call

Brother Jon

The Father welcomes the prodigal son with open arms. And when we go through Mary ". . .never was it known that anyone who fled to thy protection, implored they help or sought thy intercession was left unaided."
Memorare of St.Bernard of Clairvaux.

I am telling my story for this book after having first turned down the offer some months ago. Even though I was part of the group that brainstormed the idea for the book, I was going through a period of temptation regarding my vocation. Since then, I have been strengthened by God's grace to reject these temptations, hopefully, once and for all. We know the devil never rests, so he will keep after me; but I have come to believe that the Lord has called me to the priesthood for His reasons, and I should stop, by questioning myself, really questioning Him!

In 1943 I came into being as a child of God baptized in the Catholic Church. I knew I was a child of God early on because I was very much enamored

243

of God and strongly believed in His love for me. I was the oldest of five children: three brothers and a sister who was born when I was nineteen!

Why was I enamored of God even as a six year old? In retrospect I know that this attraction was due to the whole idea of God's being so loving of everyone. Certainly I must be included in that number. By the time I was in catechism class for my First Communion, I was drawn to the priests and made an early decision that I wanted to be a priest someday. I loved my Baltimore Catechism. I loved memorizing the lines. I loved praying. I played at saying the Mass, constructed an altar, and made my little brother serve.

I remember my First Communion day very well, though this has been 60 years past. My mother was and is very much a practicing Catholic as was her mother, my Nana, with whom I spent much time as a child, even well into my teens. They were of Italian ancestry. My father, a baptized Methodist, came from an Irish family. He was considerate of our Catholic upbringing, which was the way all mixed marriages were lived out in those days.

I went to public schools because my father couldn't afford to send me to Catholic schools. He would have if it had been possible. I was an innocent young boy, somewhat small and frail for my age, and rather quiet. I think I suffered from what later would be called an inferiority complex and this feeling of inferiority was why I kept a fairly low profile. Early on I had a strong liking for reading, especially history.

I had a strong artistic talent. Throughout my

primary schooling, I could draw and illustrate with pencils and charcoal. I can remember comparing my drawings to those of others and uttering my first words of criticism about their work as in the sky is not a blue stripe across the top of the paper;it goes all the way down to the ground.

From elementary school until my early teens, I drew pictures of the Virgin Mary and the Sacred Heart. I never quite got the Blessed Mother's face right, even though I had a great devotion to her. When I was around ten or twelve, I used to ride my bicycle to St. Mary's Church, and I would pray before her statue in the parish Lourdes Grotto. I would look over at the statue of St. Bernadette kneeling a few feet away and want to identify with her as loved in the same way as she was by the Blessed Mother. I remember going to confession even every week when I was twelve and trying to figure out what to say. I just liked to be in the Church on Saturday afternoons and at the grotto afterwards.

I remember noticing girls probably around the second and third grade and thought they were generally very special. I identified them as being sweet for the most part and wanted them to appreciate me. At the same time I remember feeling somewhat inadequate because of my stature (I was already considered somewhat puny). Only the nicest and shyest girls paid attention to me. This continued well on into high school.

And then came the 'fall" around the sixth grade. In my innocence, I became influenced by some same-aged male cousins who took me aside and told me about the "usefulness" of girls. The actual experience of what they meant took me another six or seven years to find out for myself, but I distanced myself from that innocent desire for God. As I grew into my teens, this admiration for girls changed from noticing their sweetness to noticing their other attributes, and maybe even to having a preference that they be less sweet. Now, when going to Confession, I no longer needed to wonder what I would say to the priest. At this point, the priesthood had become one of the furthest things from my mind, although I know today that I still held priests in high regard.

In high school I dated infrequently. I don't remember ever going steady, but I always wanted to sit near the prettiest girls in class. By now I was 5' 9" and twenty pounds underweight so I was no longer considered 'puny', but I also was not 'cute'".

I had become very good in drawing and illustrating, adept especially at drawing the human form and animals. I could make a tree look like a tree. My interest was limited to these forms; I did not like to draw houses or landscapes. I never took any formal training other than high school art classes, but I enjoyed the attention that my art work got me. And many of these drawings were in the margins of my notebooks. Those sitting nearby sometimes got into trouble for admiring my work instead of listening to the teacher. All of these drawings indicate how much I wanted attention, especially from girls.

After high school I didn't want to go to college, much to my father's chagrin. For a year I worked at low–paying, clerical type jobs. Then I decided to go to a state university because some of my new friends had decided to enroll, and I wanted to go with them. I wanted to run with the guys. All this time I still went to Sunday Mass, not just because my mother made me, but because I realized it was the right thing to do. I even thought I owed it to God to go to Confession occasionally.

College didn't work out. I lasted one semester and spent much of the time in a pool hall and dating a couple of college girls. By now I was two inches taller, twenty pounds heavier, and apparently cuter.

I didn't know what I wanted to do with my life, but the priesthood wasn't even on the radar screen. Even though I was still going to Mass every Sunday, I no longer viewed it as central. It was more like a custom and only vaguely now the right thing to do.

I had trouble finding a job when I left after that one semester because I was considered to be less than steady. So I found myself in the downtown recruiter's office. I wanted to join the navy. I even took all the tests and passed them. Then, being the follower that I was, I listened to a friend who had quit the same college and was going into the navy with me. Together we took a two week trip around the state before we were due to report. He talked me into touring the state parks on one final, girl–chasing spree. The night we returned, when we were due to report the next morning, he announced he was not going to go. Being a follower, I also dropped the plan. We had not yet been sworn in. Boy, was the naval recruiter upset with me. A week later I joined the air force, afraid to go back to that navy recruiter, my first choice.

During the three years and eight–plus months I was in the air force I saw San Antonio, Nebraska, and Newfoundland. I escaped the Vietnam War even though the air force gave me a ribbon to wear on my chest to signify I had been in the service during the war. They gave one to everyone.

The big event of my air force time was getting married. The girl was the last one I had dated, just briefly, before going into the service. We were married in the Church, against the better judgment of the priest, after knowing each other only ten months. Most of the courtship was letter writing. Even before the marriage I had stopped practicing my faith.

My wife and I produced two beautiful children who were proof of the good God gave us, even though we gave each other hell. We lasted together eleven years. Thirty-five years later I sought and secured an annulment because I wanted to enter religious life!

After the air force and over the next thirty-five years, I held seven or eight different jobs with as many companies. I used my training to secure jobs in areas of management and sales. Three years after the divorce, I married again, of course, outside the Church. There were no children, but the children of my first marriage, originally in my first wife's custody, later came to me and my second wife. They were now ages thirteen and eleven years old. After twelve years of this second marriage, which I never took seriously enough to be faithful to, my wife and I agreed to divorce.

During all of this time I didn't practice my faith. However, I know now that I still had some kind of vague connection to Our Lord, and I believe that this was entirely the work of the Blessed Virgin Mary. I knew I was living a terrible life. I severely damaged the lives of two women and my children. The afternoon of the second divorce, upon leaving the court house, I broke down. The words came to mind: When was the last time you were happy? The answer came immediately: When I loved God!

I realized then that I had to stop being what I had been and go back to the Church. The journey back began at that very moment, but it took a somewhat circuitous route. I started going back to Mass but not to Communion because I knew I was in mortal sin and I was afraid to go to Confession.

I began to pray the Rosary and pray to Our Lady Refuge of Sinners. In my mind, I was the greatest of them all! However, the evil one, who doesn't want to lose you because he has you, was adept at making me believe I could have God and my sins. I thought this arrangement was okay if the sin involved someone I wanted to love.

My conscience bothered me, of course. I still wasn't going to Confession. Then I realized that this situation wasn't right and went to Confession. Receiving the sacrament helped me begin eighteen months of chastity, church going, prayer, and wondering what I should do with the rest of my life. I also tried to make up for lost time with my children.

Then, as God would have it, I met a woman I really did come to love. We saw each other for three years and chastity was not a part of the relationship. I had fallen again but believed our relationship was okay with God because I loved her. I was only compounding my sin. About six months before the end of this relationship, I realized that she didn't want to marry me.

A few weeks before the actual break-up, I read an article about the Marian apparitions at Medjugorje. I got back home and began to investigate by contacting people who might know. One of them suggested that I attend a Marian conference in a nearby city. I went. While praying the Rosary with 500 other people, it suddenly struck me that everything about the relationship with the woman I thought I loved had been all wrong, all wrong. I broke down again on the spot. I looked around and the priests had already stopped hearing Confessions. The plane ride back later that afternoon was dismal. I think I cried all the way back. The next day I could not wait to go to Confession. I made a general Confession. Then I went to the home of the woman I loved and broke off the relationship with a full explanation. She said, "I knew when you went to that conference you would make this decision." She cried. I did not. My sorrow was not for her. It was for my soul. In time, she took instructions to come into the Catholic Church. We saw each other in a platonic way and two years later she married a nice Catholic man in the Church!

At that point my reversion to God and His Church began in earnest. In the meantime, not knowing what to do with my life, I began to go to daily Mass and pray the Rosary and do penitential weeping. This went on for two years. I began to think about giving what was left of the rest of my life completely to God. I didn't want another woman, another marriage. That was more than fifteen years ago.

The call became very strong to walk away from those aspects of my previous life. I began to investigate men's religious orders that might accept me, but I was still married in the eyes of the Church. I knew my marital status would prevent me from joining any established orders. There were, however, many new societies that would only require promises. An annulment would not be required or demanded since these groups were not officially recognized even by the Bishop.

This was the way I thought I would have to go because an annulment after thirty-five years seemed unlikely. During this search I became involved in a lay apostolate of a well-established men's pontifical order right in my home town. They trained me theologically, and I began to speak at parishes and conferences.

Three of the new orders accepted me after visits, but I ended up turning them down, not knowing really why. During this time, I decided I needed to try to get the annulment. I am not even sure why, it just seemed imperative. So I applied. Thirty-five years is indeed a long time. I prayed a great deal, always full of doubt that my efforts could ever be successful. I needed three witnesses. Two of these were so unlikely that, eventually, I had to see their testimony as a part of my call to the priesthood. My annulment came through in half of the average time it usually took in that diocese.

Upon receipt of the annulment, I telephoned a priest of the community I had been working with asking for direction for my life. To my great surprise he said, "Why don't you join us." I was fifty-nine! The vocations' director only agreed to accept me as an aggregate to the community without formal vows. I agreed completely, believing this was the way God wanted me in religious life. Seven months later, after living with the community, they offered me vows as a brother. Five months later, I was in the novitiate. I still only wanted to be a brother, and this had been the understanding when the community accepted me. I did not feel in any way that I should press God to go beyond being a religious brother.

The year prior to my final vows, having done some college courses, I began to think in terms of the priesthood again.

Fifty years after my first call, I got my last call!

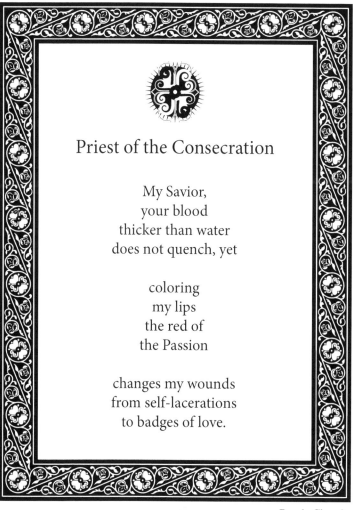

Priest of the Consecration

My Savior,
your blood
thicker than water
does not quench, yet

coloring
my lips
the red of
the Passion

changes my wounds
from self-lacerations
to badges of love.

Ronda Chervin

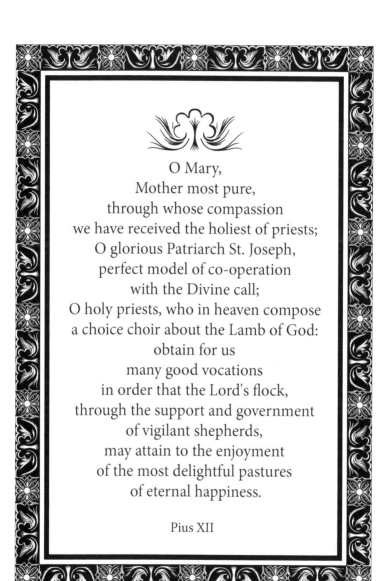

O Mary,
Mother most pure,
through whose compassion
we have received the holiest of priests;
O glorious Patriarch St. Joseph,
perfect model of co-operation
with the Divine call;
O holy priests, who in heaven compose
a choice choir about the Lamb of God:
obtain for us
many good vocations
in order that the Lord's flock,
through the support and government
of vigilant shepherds,
may attain to the enjoyment
of the most delightful pastures
of eternal happiness.

Pius XII

Priest of Purgatory

Might the final task of our priest be,
to hang nooses around our necks.
A 'baptized co-dependency'
is his, as he drags along
his captive-flock,
in his sacerdotal triumph
along the paths of purgatory,
through the pearly arches.

Ronda Chervin

Dear Lord,
Give us good priests,
shepherds after Thy own Heart,
to adorn Thy Church with holiness,
to guide Thy people with wisdom and charity,
to offer with great reverence the Sacrifice of the Mass,
to strengthen the faith of believers,
to bring the truth to those who do not yet believe,
to preach with humility the Gospel of Christ,
to bring forgiveness to sinners,
to give to the humble the Bread of Life,
to comfort the sorrowing,
to relieve the suffering,
to strengthen the dying,
to pray for the dead,
to shed light in the darkness,
and in all things to imitate our Lord Jesus Christ,
the Son of God and Son of Mary.
Amen.

Fr. Fabian Duggan, OSB

FRVCTVM·SVVM·DABIT
IN·TEMPORE·SVO

"I Paul, am already being poured out like a libation… I have competed well, I have run the race, I have kept the faith… The Lord stood by me and gave me strength, so that through me the proclamation might be completed and all the people might hear it…"

What a beautiful way to describe the life of the priest – *"I am being poured out like a libation."* This is also an image from the Roman pagan religions of the time. In honor of the gods, when people would take their toast and drink their wine, they would always pour out one goblet of wine for the god onto the ground. In a way, it was wasted, it was the portion no one else could have, it belonged to the god. St. Paul takes this image and applies it to himself, and to the Christian priesthood. The priest is the libation to the True God. His is the life that in a sense is "wasted" as far as the world is concerned because it is not used for anything else but to be poured out in service to God and His Church.

And the priest's life and work are not over until he has poured himself out fully, like Christ the Lord, giving the last drop. But for the priest and the Church, this is no waste. Though the world finds the Catholic priesthood unintelligible, for the Church it is a celebration. Never to hold back, always to give; never to be stingy, always to pour out generously; never to say "for me," always to be "for others." This is the priesthood, this is what Christ sets as the pattern to be imitated, this is how he builds his Church.

May the Lord Jesus continue to call forth new apostles to take up the stole and chasuble, the shield of faith and sword of the Spirit, and go forth with joy to the ends of the earth, vanquishing the gates of hell, and establishing God's Kingdom in its stead.

Fr. Glen Mullan

CHRISTUS NASCITURUS

FIRST WORD
OF THE
LAST CALL

For further information concerning
late vocations, contact
Holy Apostles College and Seminary
33 Prospect Hill Road
Cromwell, CT 06416=2027:
www.holyapostles.edu/seminary

Order copies of LAST CALL from
ccwatershed.org/lastcall
createspace.com
amazon.com

Visit Dr. Chervin's websites:
rondachervin.com
spiritualityrunningtogod.com

Read her blogs on Rondaview:
ccwatershed.org

Pray for vocations, early and late.

Made in the USA
San Bernardino, CA
12 June 2013